FUNdamentals
in Family Life

by

Jerry Nance PhD

&

Joe Phillips

Scripture quotations marked (NLT) are taken from the Holy Bible, New Living Translation, copyright © 1996, 2004, 2007 by Tyndale House Foundation. Used by permission of Tyndale House Publishers, Inc., Carol Stream, Illinois 60188. All rights reserved.

Cover design by Ben Steffens.

ISBN 13: 978-1539366874
ISBN 10: 1539366871

Printed by Color House Graphics, Grand Rapids, MI USA.

To order additional copies of this book, contact:
Teen Challenge International—Southeast Region
15 West 10th Street
Columbus, GA 31901
Phone: 706-596-8731
Email: cttaccounts@teenchallenge.cc

Published by
Jeryl Lynn Nance
15 W. 10th Street
Columbus, GA 31901

Table of Contents

ABOUT THE AUTHORS

Jerry Nance PhD

PRESIDENT / CEO

TEEN CHALLENGE SOUTHEAST REGION

and

GLOBAL TEEN CHALLENGE

For over 31 years Dr. Jerry Nance has worked with Teen Challenge ministries in various leadership roles. He served on staff with David Wilkerson at World Challenge where he was an instructor at the first Teen Challenge staff training school and also served on David Wilkerson's Crusade staff. Dr. Nance was the founder of Miami Outreach Ministries, a women's crisis center. In 1991, he became the President/CEO of Teen Challenge of Florida Inc., which at the time consisted of one rented facility in the orange groves of Winter Haven, Florida. Under Jerry's leadership, Teen Challenge has grown to include 20 residential centers in six states.

In 2006, Dr. Nance was asked to serve as the President/CEO of Global Teen Challenge which provides leadership and training tools for Teen Challenge leaders and programs around the world. Since that time, Global Teen Challenge has grown from having centers in 82 nations to now being in 115 nations. Over 1,400 Teen Challenge programs are served by the staff of Global Teen Challenge.

Dr. Nance also serves on the Teen Challenge USA Board of Directors and is an advocate for mentoring, training, coaching and releasing young leaders for the work of Teen Challenge.

Dr. Nance has authored several books including *Dream to Reality* and *Core Values,* which are used extensively in Teen Challenge programs around the world, and *Finding the Fun in Fundraising.* Dr. Nance and his wife Libby are proud to be the parents of three grown children and are blessed with nine grandchildren.

Joe Phillips

PRESIDENT / CEO

JPM

JOE PHILLIPS MINISTRIES

 Joe Phillips is an evangelist, comedian, actor and author of *The Third Chair: Implementing Lasting Change*. Joe has enjoyed a variety of ministry experiences over the last few decades. For fifteen years he served three large churches in the Southeast as lead student-ministry pastor. Joe has done missions work in Jamaica, Paraguay, Argentina, Honduras, Venezuela, Nicaragua, Brazil, Malaysia, Singapore, Thailand and Moldova. He has been a missionary to adolescent Teen Challenge students, a lead pastor in West Virginia, and a denominational state youth director in Georgia. He has been outreach director of parachurch organizations, a coach and athletic director. For ten years Joe has traveled as an evangelist, preaching in churches, camps, campaigns, conferences and conventions. He uses stand-up comedy as a tool to reach people at fundraisers and outreaches. For five years Joe has played the part of Ebenezer Scrooge in *A Christmas Carol* and in an adaptation he calls the "Ebenezer Experience." There have been forty performances in seven states, with 22,000 people in attendance. Every show has ended with a presentation of the Gospel and people have come to know the Lord in every one—more than 300 people, in fact. Joe and Cecilia have four children and one grandchild and live outside Charlotte, NC.

Website: joephillipsministries.com
Facebook: Joe Phillips Ministries
Twitter: @revrollinjoe

INTRODUCTION

Jerry

Life is filled with so many wonderful opportunities to grow, learn and laugh. Over the years we all have practiced principles in our lives and homes that help us as individuals or as families to take some pressure off, relax and just laugh. These FUNdamental principles build our impressions of family life and impact us for life. Why not focus on the Fun in the Fundamentals. Over these next pages I trust some of the principles that we used will be of help to you in establishing your own fundamental principles for your family.

I have solicited the help of Joe and Cecilia Phillips to give their input on how they too found fun in family life. Joe and Cecilia Phillips have served as youth pastors, lead pastors, and evangelists for more than 25 years, raising four wonderful children. I solicited their help so you could get a broader base of input when deciding what principles you might want to apply to your personal life and family life. There is not one way to do the journey of life as a family; there are many ways to find fun in family life. I pray that these stories and principles help you as you navigate your family through life, and result in new traditions and amazing memories for you, your children and grandchildren.

Finding fun in the fundamentals of family life is not difficult. There are so many funny things that happen along the way of dating, marriage, having kids, raising kids and our work experiences. It's just important to keep everything in proper perspective.

Seriously, Laugh—Family life affords much to laugh about!

Take a moment right now and think of some of the funny things that have happened in your home, with your family, or things that have happened at work or in a relationship that you laugh about every time you think of the event. I hope those memories bring a smile to your own face as you begin reading this book.

What family or relationship memories make you laugh?

I believe we all have some really funny memories that bring smiles and warm feelings when we remember those family moments. Even for some of you who may have had a really tough home environment, think hard and find a few good moments, memories and dwell on that and work hard to get past the hardships that occurred. God will help you.

For those of you who are single, reading this book:
Don't believe the lie that "marriage is not worth the commitment!"

I happen to believe the deepest levels of joy and fulfillment in life come because we make deep commitments, such as "till death do us part." We then do our best to live those words out to the fullest in our relationships. I know those words have fallen short in many instances, but that should not be a license for our kids to live together rather than commit to marriage.

For those of you who are married, understand this:
No family is perfect!

- Great families take a lifetime of commitment! Those commitments bring the results that make it well worth the investment of time, energy and effort.

- Selfishness is the greatest enemy for you to contend with in your marriage and family. Deal with your own selfishness first and it will be much easier on you.

- Fulfillment in relationships is the result of *we*, not *I*.

Please know this book is not a how-to book as much as it simply serves as a resource tool with living examples of ideas and principles that have worked in two families and stood the test of time through many challenges and multiple moves. We have lived by convictions and values and applied those to our lives and it has helped make the difference for us.

Making memories and building a sense of home, family and love are critical to truly enjoying life and having a place to turn when life offers up its challenges.

Committing time to your family will pay big dividends as you put into action some of the ideas and suggestions that have emerged from the stories in this book.

As a single person, you witness the interaction of your own family and the families around you. Consider the positive characteristics you see in others and begin to apply some of those characteristics to your own family life. The same is true for those of us who are married. We too can watch, spend time with other families and experience their interaction with one another and observe the characteristics that impress us. It's okay to borrow the customs of other families and apply them to your own.

There is no patent on how to have fun in a family.
Find what looks fun and try it.

I have learned over the years that not everyone had good role models when they were growing up and really don't have a baseline to draw from of what normal family life looks like. Others had such horrific home lives that in spite of not wanting to see their own family or children experience what they experienced they default back to some of the very behaviors that caused their own pain.

There is hope! There are good family models we can draw from. Again, let me say that there is no such thing as a perfect family, but we have the opportunity to work on building our families and developing customs, habits and rituals that make life special and fun for our families. We can learn to be better parents, husbands, wives, and role models in our homes. It takes work and it goes against this self-centered culture we live in, but in the end it is worth it.

Here are some of our funny, real-life stories that I hope raise some fun memories from your own family.

Nance Family Safari

My family and I went to Waco, Texas, to visit my wife's parents. While we were there my father-in-law suggested we visit a new attraction in Waco, which was a drive-thru safari with a variety of African wildlife. We enthusiastically decided to go, and let me tell you this is one family outing our family has enjoyed reliving for years. The problem is that it was at my personal expense. Let me explain.

First, we drove through the gate and were given the opportunity to buy food for the animals. I was excited to buy a bag so I could draw the animals to the car for an up-close look. I had my bag in hand in the front seat ready to attract the animals.

As soon as we entered the gate we had wildebeest, waterbucks, giraffes and other African species headed our way. I rolled the car window down, planning to toss some food on the ground so we could watch them eat next to our car. But before I could do that, a large antelope stuck its head through the window looking for food. It happened so fast I couldn't stop it. I was panicking as I tried to figure out how to get his head out of my face. In addition, he was drooling a flood of saliva all over my arm! I reacted by throwing the whole bag of food out the window to get the animal away from me. In a flash the entire bag of food was gone. Thankfully, he went for the food, but he had done his damage. My arm was covered with saliva slime.

As I grabbed every napkin and paper towel I could find to wipe the mess off my arm, a giraffe approached the car and began to eat the rubber off the windshield wipers. Our kids were laughing so hard they were crying! They couldn't stop laughing as they told and retold the story over and over again. All I could do was laugh with them and keep wiping.

And that was just the first few moments of our safari adventure!

Next, we headed to a part of the park where we could get out and walk around and see other animals. I was drawn to a cage where an orangutan named Clyde was sitting. The plaque on his cage said he had been in the movie *Every Which Way but Loose*, starring Clint Eastwood. I had seen that movie and wanted to get a close-up look at Clyde. I was amazed by the size of his hands and even the size of each knuckle. I stood there for a few minutes observing him and thinking about his life in captivity. He was curious too, I guess, because he moved toward me, took hold of the bars and pulled himself up to the front of the cage. We stood there in a face-off, then all of a sudden he spit at me! I jumped back, trying to avoid it, but to no avail. A big glob of saliva hung on the front of my shirt.

In no time at all, I'd been drooled on by an antelope and spit on by an orangutan!

Of course, my kids stood there laughing and getting more enjoyment from this than they should have. To save what little dignity I had left, I did what any real man would do: I worked up my own wad of spit and blew it back on Clyde then got out of range in a hurry, fearing what else he might throw at me. Our kids were having the time of their lives; me, not so much.

We left there and went to the reptile section of the park. I'm no fan of snakes, but they're secured in terrariums, right? Of course. But as I stepped up to a large box with a Plexiglas front to look inside, the glass boomed beside my leg when a great big rattlesnake hit the glass, fangs bared. I nearly jumped out of my antelope-slimed, orangutan-spit upon skin, and high-stepped it out of there to get as far away from that snake as I could. Thank God the glass between me and that crazy reptile held its own. But that was it! My safari was over. I had been drooled on, spit on and stricken at, all in less than 30 minutes.

That was my "Alpha and Omega"—the first and the last—US-based safari I ever went on. There's a similar park near the home where I live now, but I don't plan to go anytime soon. My kids have never forgotten and continue to enjoy how Dad did safari. To this day we can't mention that trip without the entire family bursting into laughter. And though I was the brunt of every joke that day, it warms my heart to know what great memories were created from that one visit to an animal park in Waco, Texas.

Joe

It was a good day in April, 1986, when my new boss said, "I'd like you to meet our associate pastor, Jerry Nance, and this is his wife, Libby." I was single at the time and the new youth pastor. That introduction would lead to a lifelong friendship. I had been born-again for just over three years. By the prevenient grace of God I found myself in a South Florida church of more than 800 persons. I did the math and discovered I had about 1.83 days of Christian living experience for every person in that congregation. I was a sponge. I wanted to learn everything I could about everything I could, because I felt like I knew nothing. Three months after I met Jerry and Libby, I married Cecilia, my girlfriend of four years. After we were married, my bride and I would often go to Jerry and Libby's house following Sunday night service. It was much more convenient to go to their nice home than our small apartment. They had furniture to sit on! Plus, they had three small kids to put to bed.

It was in Jerry's living room that I first learned the power of the "clicker." He was the first person I ever saw mute the commercials. When I saw him do that I think I heard the angels sing. Behold, it hath forevermore been my practice to mute the commercials. But believe me, I picked up a lot more than that at the Nance house. I saw Jerry navigate bedtime for their children. I was an only child so multiple humans with multiple bedtimes, living in one house, was new territory for me. I watched Jerry and Libby pray with Denee', Kristi and Dustin before they went to sleep. I learned the way the kids negotiated for just one more glass of water and fifteen more minutes of television. Libby had such a disarming, gentle way of mothering her kids. We enjoyed those times very much, and now to be invited to participate in this project is truly an honor.

Our upbringing often forges the track that will guide our future mores, norms, policies, practices and decisions. You'll read in this book about the tremendous legacy that Jerry Nance had growing up. That upbringing forged him to be the father and grandfather he is today. Libby had an excellent legacy as well. My history is different. Here are a few highlights of my childhood. I don't wish to violate the mandate of Ephesians 6:1, so I want to speak honorably about my parents. To do less has no value. Nevertheless, I believe the facts about my history are important to the reader because not everyone was raised in a home like Jerry. You may not have been loaded into the family sedan for Sunday worship. You may not have been taught the principle of tithing. It could be that on your block, your family put the "unction" in dysfunction. My history is not typical, but it was certainly dysfunctional.

The D in Dysfunction

Get ready to meet some real-life characters with some pretty cool names. A man named Loye got a girl named Glenola pregnant in a barn in Wisconsin, from what I have been told. Glenola had a couple of serious mental illnesses that have since been diagnosed. In the early 1960s, unwed pregnancy was not smiled upon. When the news began to be whispered that "Sue was in trouble," Loye was instructed by his family to go to Montana until the deed was done— namely my birth. It was a "head for the hills, a baby is on the way" situation. The story goes that Glenola's sister, Zelphia Madonna, talked her out of getting an abortion, which was illegal at the time. Madonna said, "Give the kid a chance. Who knows what it might become." I am very grateful for that conversation. Even though Glenola felt she would never get a man if she was dragging a kid around, she chose not to abort. She raised me for three years while living with her parents, Clessie and Ola. I recently learned from Glenola Sue that my grandmother Ola despised the thought of having a "brat kid" in the house. "I raised my eleven kids (give or take as my memory serves me) and you've brought this kid in my house? How dare you!" I often show on the screen at conferences one of the only pictures of my early childhood. Ola is holding a white purse and looking at me with utter disdain. I lived with her for just over three years and don't have a single memory of her. Sometimes God gives us good forgetters.

On the other hand my grandfather, Clessie Rollin, was as cool as the other side of the pillow. I remember him well. They told him he had to give me up. He would never live to see me graduate from high school, they prophesied. He reluctantly agreed to sign papers. But when I graduated from high school, the front door of my little mill house in Georgia opened up and Clessie Rollin Mills walked into Rollin Joe's gathering and loudly exclaimed, "I'm alive!"

So with a judge's signature in 1967, my first cousin, Gordon Wayne Phillips, became my dad and his twenty-one-year-old wife, Elizabeth, became my mom. My mom became my aunt. My aunt became my grandmother. My grandparents became my great-grandparents. Is it any wonder that math has always been challenging to me? I can barely understand my family tree. It looks like shrubbery.

My biological mother actually told me she used to put me in the attic to terrorize me. She said, "I would make scary sounds when you cried." My adopted mother told me a couple of years ago that when they tried to bathe me following the adoption I would scream bloody murder, scream like I was being water-boarded. I grew up unwanted, abused and scared. Then I was rescued. I was adopted. I have been twice adopted!

Life was good and, in fact, great from the age of three until fifteen. I was given a red wagon at six years old. I was given a green, five-speed bike when I was ten. My new dad changed my life the day he put a basketball goal in concrete when I was twelve. I would go on to play four years of basketball for two colleges because Dad did that. Dad gave me a blue, fiberglass canoe when I was fourteen so I could fish for white bass on the Lake of the Ozarks.

Jesus was not a point of emphasis through those years. I have a visitor's letter somewhere from a Baptist church in Big Spring, TX, that was sent when I was a very small boy. I have no memory of the church. I do remember the Collet Church of the Nazarene in Portland, IN. I remember VBS, in particular. I remember standing up and joining the church with my new mom, Elizabeth. Even so, the whole church deal didn't really take. We moved to Missouri, and my folks let me go to the Presbyterian Church in Chillicothe with family friends. I did that for about three years. In fact, the first sermon I ever preached was on a Sunday morning, in that church, when I was thirteen. I still have the four index cards titled, "Jesus Can Be Your Best Friend." He wasn't mine. I didn't know him. The church was just desperate for a youth to speak on Youth Sunday. Five years later I was dramatically born again on a dance floor in a nightclub in Columbus, GA. That's another story for another time.

My father and mother divorced when I was fifteen years old. I was shocked because there was not a hint of trouble that I ever detected in our home. Again, not to dishonor but to inform, about a week after my mother left the small duplex we lived in, a new woman and her two small children came to live with us. I became very confused and embittered. I hope that thumbnail sketch gives a glimpse at the profound difference between the backgrounds of Dr. Nance and me.

Cecilia and I have three fantastic children ... and another one. Just kidding. I blatantly stole that joke from comedian Brian Regan. In fact, all four of our children are fantastic. As of this writing our oldest son, Joseph, is a teaching pastor at Center City Church in the heart of Charlotte, NC. He is a brilliant writer and excellent communicator. He married a school teacher four years ago and they gave us our first grandchild last month. Our oldest daughter, Lauren, teaches art and Bible classes at Concord First Assembly Academy in North Carolina. She has a unique ability of relating to the oldest person in the room and the youngest. Her heart is as big as the ocean. Our youngest son, Kennon, is a finance and accounting major at Southeastern University. He is incredibly disciplined financially and in other aspects of his life. He has gone three years and counting, age seventeen to twenty, without drinking carbonated drinks or tea. He is disciplined in the gym as well. He is resourcefully working his way through university. Madeline, our youngest daughter, is also at Southeastern. I suppose Southeastern University has turned into a family thing. Joseph and I graduated from there. Maddie is a double major in practical ministries and history. Two weeks ago she preached on a preaching team at an R.V. park and won twelve people to Jesus (not keeping score but evangelist Daddy only saw seven that day). She was born with a serious diagnosis that put her in three hospitals with a dire prognosis her first month of life. God worked a miracle for us, and not only does she not have predicted brain damage, but she excels in every way. She was in the top three academically in her private school for the SAT test—the 1,800-and-over club. She starred in multiple performances of *Annie Get Your Gun*, singing fourteen songs. As a child she was the Appalachian District Junior Bible Quiz champion. As a high schooler she won the North Carolina competition for "preaching," not once but twice. I sound like "that dad" but I am boasting in the Lord. He took a boy from a dysfunctional family and showed Himself strong in my children, and for that I boast in the Lord. He is the same yesterday as He is today. No matter what the current situation looks like, God has a marvelous way of resetting the screen. Indeed, the Lord makes beauty from ashes.

I've had many exciting things happen in my life over the last several decades. I include the honor of working on this project among the highest honors. Nothing is closer to me than knowing that my family serves the Lord and is healthy in their walk with Jesus.

CHAPTER 1

BUILDING FAMILY TRADITIONS
AND MEMORIES

Jerry

There are all kinds of family traditions that we grow up with. Some of these traditions bring a smile to our faces and even a sense of security, and then we think of other memories and they may bring the thought, "I'm not going to do that to my kids."

As a child there were things my parents did every year for the holidays that we grew to expect and later appreciate. Though I grew up in a loving Christian home, there were other things I decided I did not want to duplicate in my own home.

Let me share just a few traditions that have brought great memories to Libby and me and our kids.

Family Vacations

What does a successful vacation look like? What do you do and where do you go? The answer is different for every family, but there are some traditions families have followed that I believe could provide fresh ideas for your own vacation. The location is just a matter of convenience, cost and interest to your family.

I made the decision early on in my career to block out a minimum of two weeks vacation time so I could truly relax and get the rest I need. This has been my conviction and we have lived by it for 30 years. We usually went the last week in May and the first week in June so the kids would be out of school and before camp and other summer activities started.

I have set up some guidelines to assure I get that rest. For instance, I don't take business calls and I don't check my emails. Instead, I ask my administrative assistant to manage my calls and emails and I ask my executive staff to manage the business. I have instructed them not to call unless there is a dire emergency. I empower my staff with the authority to make decisions on my behalf and press on. This gives me the rest my mind needs and it also empowers my leadership team to learn to make decisions without me.

I give my wife my cell phone and she checks calls and texts to see if there is anything I need to address. My administrative assistant lets those who contact my office know I'm out for two weeks. She only sends my wife emails that are extremely time sensitive or truly urgent. My staff has been so faithful not to call unless it is truly urgent. This practice has worked for me. My wife and kids get all my attention for two weeks, and I come back to work rested, refreshed and ready to go at it again. It serves me like a mini sabbatical.

We also try to go to the same location each year, which helps me relax quicker. If we know where the restaurants, shopping and entertainment is, we tend to relax quicker. It is work to find the right restaurants, entertainment venues, and things to do that will entertain our kids. We found that if we go to the same place, our kids jump right into vacation routine and develop their own traditions for how they entertain themselves.

I also have developed a habit of taking my watch off and laying it aside for the entire two weeks. Imagine running hard for months on end, then not having a watch or cell phone for two weeks. It's freedom at its best. You gotta try it. I confess it's tough the first day or so, but soon I am reminded what life is like without worrying about the time. It's like being set free from an addiction.

Some years I have a few key projects with loose ends that continue to need attention while I'm away. This makes it really difficult not to take calls and conduct business, but when that happens it's the exception, not the norm. It takes discipline to keep this tradition, but it's well worth the effort.

I have also learned to do things on vacation that keep me distracted from thinking about work. I read mystery novels with high action settings. I know if I read leadership books I'll try to apply it to the ministry and try to fix something in my mind. So I keep up with world events, read fiction or history, and get lots of rest.

One of my favorite activities is surf fishing, which really lets the wind blow through my ears and distracts me from work. I can sit all day on the beach with a fishing pole, catching fish and just enjoying the wind, the surf and God's beautiful creation. I suggest you find something you enjoy and do it long enough to stop thinking of the project or program you're working on. Libby loves to sit and read while the kids enjoy the beach and help me reel in the fish, stingrays and sharks.

One of our traditions while on vacation is to have a parents' night out where the adults go out to dinner and order pizza for the kids. When the kids were young we employed sitters for them, then as they got older we let them have the house to themselves. The kids loved it. They would play hide-and-seek indoors and enjoy a movie night. Our kids loved the run of the house and we loved the break from cooking dinner. We loved spending quality time together, having conversations without the kids around. They enjoyed it as much as we did. They talked about what they did on parents' night out for weeks after the vacation, and as future vacations approached they came up with ideas of what they would do on parents' night out.

We have favorite restaurants we always visit. The Bubble Room on Captiva Island, Cobalt's on Orange Beach, Lambert's Home of the throwed roll and others are our annual visit sites. Our kids have grown up, summer after summer, going to the same places for vacation and now we go with our kids and *grandkids* to special places for vacations. One of the great joys for Libby and me is to see our grown children making traditions of their own with their own families. They are making memories that will bind their family units together forever. That is very rewarding for us.

My family has a special memory of a vacation where Uncle Tom (Libby's sister Michelle's husband) taught my son Dustin "how to catch women." Tom was teaching Dustin to cast a fishing lure off the shore and a lady was walking the beach. They stopped to let her pass. She walked behind them, then, for no good reason, she turned around and walked right back behind them. Dustin had just swung the rod back to cast when that lady walked into the lure. The hook caught her arm and when Dustin tried to cast the hook, it went deep enough to break the skin and hook her. Her arm began to bleed, and because the hook was so deep Tom couldn't remove the lure. So Tom and Dustin came into the house with this lady connected to the rod and I was then tasked to cut the line and take her to the emergency room. Uncle Tom taught Dustin how to catch women alright. And years later I ask myself, why did I have to take her to the hospital? I should have made Uncle Tom take on that little four-hour task. Then guess whose homeowners insurance paid for the doctor visit. You got it, mine.

Another wonderful memory we have as a family is when one of my dear friends, Dennis Griffin, who has since passed away, invited us to join his family in Yosemite National Park. For years, Dennis and his family got friends across the state of California to help them make calls to book dates and reserve certain sites on the opening booking day for Yosemite. Their family lived for that week every summer. Dennis planned like no one I had ever met for that week at Yosemite. He made hash brown potatoes and froze them, planned all the meals, tweaked his cooking equipment and got his RV ready for that one week every summer. It was such a privilege to be invited to join them one year. My family and I arrived at Yosemite to find a pop-up camper for Libby and me and a tent set up for our kids and their friends. Dennis had a campsite that was a masterpiece in the park.

One of their treasured trips each year was to stoke Half Dome, a 5,000-foot climb to the top of the famed granite rock formation, which would take the better part of a day. Somehow I was talked into stoking Half Dome with them, which meant hiking up the backside of the half dome for hours when I had done no training for such an adventure. My daughter Kristi really wanted to go, so I finally agreed. We rose early in the morning to make the five-hour hike.

Most memorable was the last 400 feet of the climb, which is ridiculously steep and high. You ascend to the summit, at a nearly-vertical angle, on the infamous Half Dome cables, which is like a rope ladder with wood steps on which you pull yourself up the face of the mountain. Let me tell you, it was the most challenging—and scariest—part of the adventure.

When I finally reached the top of the Dome, I could do nothing but lie on my back and try to suck in some oxygen. I was exhausted, and the air was so thin I could hardly breathe. I was glad to be there but I had no energy to get up and enjoy the sights. It was only when I saw my daughter sitting with her feet dangling off the 5,000-foot-high face of the mountain that I was motivated to move. She made me a nervous wreck. Every part of me wanted to hold on for dear life as I looked over the edge, and there she was, dangling her feet over the side. It still scares me even now as I write this. I have never liked heights, and I liked them even less with Kristi sitting precariously close to the edge of that mountain.

True, it was a breathtaking view from that height. In the distance we could see a rainstorm moving in, and lightning was hitting the mountains near us. We could see evidence, in the very place we were sitting, of years of lightning strikes, and that was all the motivation I needed to get off that rock. We took off with "lightning" speed and hiked back down to our campsite. By the time we got there my feet had blisters on top of blisters. The pain was intense, and for the rest of the day I sat on a float in a cold stream, dangling my feet in the water.

In spite of the negatives, it was an amazing experience. Kristi and I made a lasting memory and we even got a T-shirt to prove we stoked the Dome. Both Denee' and Dustin made the trip up to the top of the dome the next day. This was a badge of honor for us that lasted long past that week of camping. Even now, whenever a discussion of our week at Yosemite comes up, our stoking the Dome is always part of the conversation. What a great memory.

In addition to scheduled vacations, I've tried to plan time off around my speaking engagements when we are in places we might want to go as a family. For example, on one occasion I was speaking in Alaska and took my family. We had an opportunity to go white-water rafting down a river that was fed by melting glaciers. We signed the waivers and were required to put on these amazingly thick, save-your-life-if-you-fall-overboard wet suits, because the glacier water is so cold it can kill you if you're exposed to it for any length of time. And we still went on that rafting trip.

We rode in a five-person raft with the guide in the middle doing most of the rowing, while we enjoyed the ride. The kids sat up front and Libby and I sat in the back. As we were leaving the shore I got the guide's attention and whispered, "If you keep my wife and me dry and soak the kids, I'll give you a big tip." As we went downriver through level three and four rapids, our kids were getting absolutely soaked while Libby and I stayed wonderfully dry. We were so enjoying the trip. Finally, Kristi noticed this and asked the guide, "Hey, did my dad tell you to get us wet?" The guide smiled and said, "Yep, he offered me a big tip." She then said, "I'll give you a kiss if you get them wet and keep us dry." The game changed and the next set of rocks in the river created a level five hole that the guide took us into. I remember literally looking up at a wall of water coming at Libby and me. When it hit, we were drenched to the bone. It's a miracle we lived to tell this story. Our kids were laughing, we were laughing, and the guide smiled with great satisfaction to know he was getting a kiss from my beautiful daughter. He got his tip and the kiss and we got a family memory we have never forgotten.

It's okay to share your favorite place with your friends if you like. It's also okay to share your blessings with others. We have had dear friends allow us to use their vacation homes for two weeks a year for many years. That's been such a blessing to our family, because we wouldn't have been able to afford to rent those vacation homes. Their generosity made it possible for our family to experience amazing vacations every summer.

As God blesses us, it's good to share those blessings with others. In fact, I believe God gives many people the ability to gain wealth, but it's not given to hoard. I believe God delights in those who are generous with their resources, giving to ministries and blessing those who serve God with their lives without any thought of worldly possessions. The joy of giving and investing in others is one of the greatest purposes of wealth.

Christmas

Christmas is one of the greatest times of the year for families to establish wonderful memories. Our tradition has always been to put up the Christmas tree on the weekend of Thanksgiving. Our kids counted on this and were always home on that weekend. The kids and I would work on the outside lights, wrapping the palm tree and lining the house and shrubbery with lights.

Then we would go inside and decorate the tree together. Some years we would cut a live tree, and other years we would purchase a tree from a lot. Whatever we did, the kids always joined me. Of course, we all preferred cutting our own. The kids loved watching me climb the tree and deciding how big to cut it. We'd haul it to the car and strap it down, which was always good for a laugh. Usually we'd get it home only to find it was too big for the spot Libby had chosen for it, so I'd have to cut more off the bottom to make it fit

And, of course, we had our traditions for decorating the tree. We would turn on Christmas music, wrap the tree in twinkling lights, then turn off all the other lights in the house and begin to trim the tree. Libby always made special Christmas treats to eat as we loaded the tree with decorations. Then we'd sit down as a family, enjoy the beautiful tree, and eat more of Libby's delicious treats. The lights, the smells, the Christmas music and the ambiance of the moment created a special and memorable time.

When the kids were young they would get their sleeping bags and camp out under the tree. They loved looking up into the middle of the tree with all its decorations and lights. When they were older and in college, they would often invite their college buddies to come over during Thanksgiving to help us decorate the house and the tree. We would share our traditions with them and they would share theirs with us. I think it made them feel at home by getting the opportunity to share their traditions. We have many fond memories of these times together.

Our tradition of wrapping gifts emerged over the years. One Christmas we purchased gifts that couldn't be easily wrapped. There was a surfboard and shotguns and things that were more easily *hidden* somewhere in the house. So we decided to use empty toilet paper rolls with notes inside telling the recipient of the gift where to look. You can imagine what the kids thought when the first toilet paper roll was unwrapped. At first they were surprised and then they laughed. But with closer inspection they saw the note and read it to find the location of a surprise. It was fun for everyone to watch their face light up and see them bolt to another part of the house to find their gift.

One of our daughters got the surfboard, which we had hidden in our closet. She read the note, ran to the master bedroom, and then screamed with excitement. We could hear her banging everything in our room as she brought her new surfboard into the family room. Our son-in-law got a shotgun, which was hidden under the couch he was sitting on. After reading his note, he got down on his hands and knees, pulled out the package and unwrapped it. And, man, was he excited. He had been sitting on top of his gift for some time and had no idea, which only added to the hilarity. Everyone enjoyed the concept so much that we've continued it as a tradition in our family. Now our grandkids are experiencing the fun. They love the idea and get so excited when they see these kinds of gifts under the tree.

We've also had Christmases where we put numbers rather than names on the really big gifts so no one knew who they were for until they opened a small box—or a toilet paper roll—to see what their number was. Only then did they know which gift was theirs.

One tradition we stay true to is that we only open one gift at a time. We start with the kids now and work around the room. We pass out all the presents, then each person opens one gift and everyone in the room gets to see what they got and share in their joy. We all ooh and aah, then move on to the next person. This slows the gift process down and everyone has the chance to rejoice over what others have gotten. Lots of hugs and kisses are given out along with the "thank yous" during this time. We have found this process to be really fun. We do allow gifts that are alike to be opened at once. There's always a race to see who can unwrap theirs the fastest. Our family likes to take the time to enjoy each other's reactions to what they get and to celebrate with them. And with all this unwrapping going on, Libby is great about putting the discarded wrapping paper in big trash bags to keep things from getting too messy.

Another tradition for our family includes a visit from Old Saint Nick. Either my son, one of my two sons-in-law or I put on the Santa suit and pay a visit to the children in our family. It's so much fun to see their faces light up and to see how they handle the man in the red suit. The young ones can be a little bit shy, while the older grandkids try to figure out if Santa is one of their uncles or if it's Paw Paw behind the beard.

The ladies all pitch in to prepare the special foods we love for the holidays. We put tables together so we can all feel we're at the same table, even if it runs into two or more rooms of the house. The kids love watching their parents, grandparents and aunts and uncles interacting together and enjoy the stories that are served along with Christmas dinner.

As I'm sure you know, little children can make a mess, and dirty diapers, nap times and other things create plenty of chaos with seventeen of us around the table. But the laughs, the fun, the traditions and the great photos far outweigh the chaos and make memories for our family that will last a lifetime.

I'll share one last idea that has become a new tradition for Libby and me. As everyone knows, it's expensive to raise a family, and there have been years when our children could only afford to buy gifts for their own children. So Libby and I decided to have each couple draw the name of another couple in the family, then give them money to buy gifts for each other. We watch the grandkids while they go last-minute shopping. It's so much fun to hear them say, "We get Target!" or "We get Dillard's!" We give them a time limit to get their shopping done to keep things exciting and moving along. It costs us a few extra dollars, but it's a blessing for them and for us.

That's finding fun in the family!

Special Events: Boys' Hunting Trip

I have always enjoyed deer hunting and have tried to take my son with me so we could have some dad/son time. My own family hunts each year in south Arkansas, and from time to time I take a trip to Arkansas to hunt with them. This gave me time with my father, brothers and brother-in-law. It has always been a great time for me and I so appreciate my wife seeing the importance of this time spent with my family. She would say, "Jerry, take Dustin and go and enjoy yourselves." We did this for years and when my sons-in-law came along, I began to take them with us to hunt. We have spent invaluable time together around campfires, sharing meals, laughing, talking about the hunt that day. Of course, there are other stories that surface around the campfire that keep us entertained. These are very rich times together building lasting memories.

On our last hunt to Arkansas, with my son and sons-in-law, we had an especially good time and lots of laughs. My brother-in-law had asked me at dinner if I would load up the remains of the deer that had been processed that day, put them on the back of a four wheeler to take to the back of the property, and dump them for the wildlife to enjoy.

That sounded easy enough. The deer guts were in a plastic, 55-gallon drum. I loaded it onto the four-wheeler and took off. That's when the fun began. I had gotten about a mile down the trail, towards the back of the property, when the four-wheeler died for no reason. I pushed the starter button and it started right up, which I was glad about, but it only went a few feet and died again. It did that several times. Now, you need to picture the setting. First of all, the night was pitch black. It was so dark I could hardly see my hand in front of my face. I thought I'd let the motor cool off a bit and try again, when I heard a sound in the distance. I knew the Arkansas Game and Fish Commission had introduced wolves back into the state, and what I believed I heard was the howling of a pack of wolves.

Remember, I was in total darkness with a full tub of blood and deer guts calling out to the wolves as sure as a dinner bell. I didn't have a gun with me or even a flashlight to guide me back to the camp. Sure, I knew the way but not in the dark, and the howls were getting closer and closer. I started the four-wheeler again and it ran another fifteen yards before it quit. I was stuck, getting nowhere fast, and fighting the panic that was trying to grip me. I was getting more terrified with each howl. I needed to decide what to do.

I dug in my pocket for my cell phone, knowing that it seldom worked that deep in the woods. But to my surprise my phone had one bar. I made my call to my friend Dan, the one person I knew was still at the camp and who I thought might have his phone with him. He swears that when I called I said, "Daaaaan, youuuuu've, gooooot tooooo come get meeeeeee! The fooooooour-wheeeeeeler is broken downnnnnn and I hear the howl of wolves. Get a gun and come right noooooooow!"

I'm sure I didn't sound that pathetic but I can tell you I was never so thankful to see a set of headlights coming up the trail to my rescue. I never did see the animals making those horrible howls, and I did take the guts on the second four-wheeler to the back of the camp, but I had a gun and someone with me for protection. The guys laughed until they cried around the campfire at Dan's version of the phone call. My son and sons-in-law were laughing and retelling the story over and over. And okay, I admit I may have sounded like a scared little boy on the phone, but I doubt any one of those guys would have been any braver had they been in my shoes.

No matter. It was a great trip, with great memories and great lessons.

Special Events: Girls' Annual Weekend

A couple of years ago my wife decided that since I was taking the boys hunting each year that she deserved to have a girls' weekend for herself, our two daughters and our daughter-in-law. Libby felt it was only fair for the girls to have time together to shop and have fun as they explored some of the cities in our region of the country. So the guys take care of the kids while she and the girls go to a bed and breakfast or a hotel for a few days, in the city of their choice. She plans out a few activities, buys them a book each year that she has read and enjoyed, but the goal is just to have fun. True, it takes some work to get everyone's schedules coordinated to make it happen, but Libby and the girls find it's truly worth the effort. They are making great memories together. And it's good for the guys to keep the kids all weekend, which helps them appreciate their wives more than they already do.

Those are some of the things the Nance family does to make memories. Here are some Phillips family traditions and ways they make memories.

Joe

Family Vacations

The reader will discover a good deal of nuanced diversity between Jerry and me regarding approaches and style on a variety of issues. The love of God and the blood of Jesus join us and all believers in unity and family. The way we set the table and the way we do so many other things are as different as the number of people there are. Fifteen years as a youth minister with four kids limits options regarding vacations. I regret poor planning regarding my family and the subject of vacations. I made excuses. "I have too much to do" and "I don't have enough money." I contend in life that we basically do what we want to with our time and money with a few obvious exceptions—our pressing responsibilities.

For my family, our two vacation strategies early on consisted of two tracks: family visits and ministry opportunities. We have so many great memories of visiting with Jimmy and Anne Griggs at 3239 Mustang Drive in Columbus, GA. A few days ago I was alone in that house preparing to move my eighty-seven-year-old mother-in-law to North Carolina with us. I experienced a different set of memories in every single room of that house. When I walked into the family room I replayed in my mind my oldest son learning to walk and navigate that six-inch step. He would walk up to the vast valley and plop down on his hind end. He would swing his little feet over the edge and then stand. He did it over and over again. Mustang Drive was not a mountain chalet, but the incredible memories in that small house are priceless. No matter where we lived as a family—the beaches of beautiful South Florida, the mountains of West Virginia, the metro area of Charlotte—a week at Nana and Papaw's was a wonderful getaway.

Our other early family strategy was to combine ministry and vacation. Budget was a major consideration, but by combining ministry and vacation we could do something exciting and it was paid for by Dad's preaching. However, I do NOT recommend this if there is a choice. Why? Because in this scenario, Dad is very distracted. There are sermons to prepare and crowds to minister to. We were together, sort of, but I was never 100% there. That wasn't fair to my family. On the other hand, the kids got to swim in some incredible places, play with some fun new friends, and see some special sights. As of this writing I have ministered in twenty "districts" or states, in 110 events. Sixty-three of those have been youth camps. There are many people who can't take their children to work. They may have a "bring-your-child-to-work day" once a year. But the ministry is often enhanced by bringing the kids to work. Phillips kids will never forget long days on the lake, in the campgrounds, or on the fields watching student competition. Nor will they forget the powerful three- and four-hour services at night. The bi-annual General Councils and conferences allowed the children to see some great American cities. Cecilia and I are certainly grateful for these opportunities. The best vacations, however, are the ones where each family member can unwind completely.

Speaking of that, for the last six years we have been blessed with some wonderful blessings like Jerry writes about. Gracious families that own beach property have opened their hearts and homes to us. We have stayed in a beautiful three-bedroom condo in Myrtle Beach, SC. A precious North Carolina family has allowed us to stay in the home they own that has been in their family for generations. It's a block from the beach, but we can park right at the door. We see the water, but we're not on the water. The home is older, but my kids love it so much because of the simple layout. Plus, the history that is special to our friends has become special to us. A Georgia friend has opened her condo in Panama City, FL. The sand is gorgeous and there are plenty of things to do and see.

When on vacation we sleep late, get the wagon ready, stake out our homestead claim in the sand, and play/nap until late afternoon. Eating out is a necessity in my business. Vacations provide us an opportunity to cook and eat all our meals in the homes where we stay, which is something we relish. There is one exception. During our vacation we eat one meal out at a good seafood restaurant. We take pictures and have the greatest time. Moving forward, vacations are going to be staples in our lives. I have an expectation for them, especially now that grandchildren are coming into the mix. Rest is Biblical. Sabbaths are theological.

Christmas and Other Holidays

Holidays are special to all families and our family is no exception. On Thanksgiving we make great food—and by "we" I mean Cecilia. It's pretty traditional Americana. Football games, food coma, laughing, pie, and more pie. Easter, at one time, was an opportunity to buy new outfits for church that Cecilia would find on sale. At some point the joy of new church clothes lost its luster as church dress codes changed. There were some years that we had Easter baskets for each of the kids.

Here is a full and complete admission from me regarding holidays. We do some nice things for a number of holidays, but at Christmas we lose our minds. Christmas is the basket we put almost all of our eggs in. It is the centerpiece. We usually buy gifts just in advance of the big day, and we do that for a couple of reasons. First, we had to keep finding the extra money! Second, we tried once, and only once, the maniacal shopping experience known as Black Friday. I've made few vows in life but I vowed never to participate in the Black Friday chaos again if the Lord would let me survive and stay out of jail. It's a vow I've had no problem keeping.

Most of our Christmas Eves began with a special church service followed by dinner at a Chinese restaurant. Our kids went to bed at an excitedly too-late hour on Christmas Eve. That late hour actually served a purpose: because they went to bed late, they got up late the next morning. Once they were asleep Cecilia and I retrieved from every hiding place the gifts we'd purchased, then we'd set up a table in our bedroom, complete with tape, scissors and wrapping paper, and have an all-night wrapping session. The Phillips children made an oath in blood not to enter "Santa's Workshop." For the last ten years my mom, Elizabeth, would come from Florida to help wrap. I'd usually give out before she did, and she and Cecilia would finish up the loose ends. After the gifts were wrapped, we'd place them under the tree, grouped by whom the gifts belonged to. Big gifts, like bicycles and such, were usually not wrapped. Thankfully, the all-nighters are behind us now, but we have great memories of those times.

As I said, the kids slept late on Christmas morning because they went to bed late on Christmas Eve. That certainly helped Mom, Dad and Grandma, because we spent the graveyard shift wrapping. The kids understood that there would be a mandatory photo shoot. Cheap pajamas were purchased and assigned the night before. When we had houses with stairs we'd position the kids on the stairs for "the picture." Following the modeling session we'd have a light and easy breakfast.

Every year I'd read the Christmas story from the second chapter of Luke before we opened gifts. We'd designate a gift "passer-outer" or two, and then we'd settle in for a long winter's event. We spent hours passing out gifts and opening them one at a time; we each paid attention to the opener. Too much work, time and treasure was invested to have it over in five minutes. We'd make a big circle and watch as one person at a time opened their gifts. We would ooh and aah over each one. Socks and shirts were at the beginning of the pass-out order, while the big gifts—or, rather, the more expensive ones— were saved for last. Sometimes it was fun to put a small, expensive gift in a large box to throw the kids off. Cecilia would help in regards to order. "Not that one yet."

When two people are married, they bring their unique upbringing into the relationship. I was raised with colored tree lights, and gifts were placed under the tree weeks before Christmas. The suspense of wondering what was in each package—and picking them up and shaking them—is a fun memory to me. Cecilia was raised differently. Her family also had colored lights, but now she prefers white lights and more elegant decorations. Gifts under the tree were from extended family members only. But the big "Santa" gifts didn't appear till Christmas morning. It was never worth arguing about to me. She just wins. I joke in some of my shows, "I wear the pants in this family … whichever ones she lays out." And "I run things at my house … I run the vacuum cleaner, the garbage disposal..."

I'll say a word about how we dealt with the Santa Claus issue. When asked by my children if Santa was real, I would tell them, "Santa is real, like a real fun game we play. He's not real like Jesus is real, but it's real fun to play." I never had negative repercussions from that. If a parent ever complained that my child said something about Santa, my out was, "We tell the kids that Santa is real and real fun. Not real like Jesus." No one ever complained, including my children.

Hospitality has been an important part of our holiday tradition throughout the years. It's one of our family's core values. In West Virginia, there was a man in special circumstances in our congregation. Lee was blind and had about six teeth in his head and those teeth were on their last legs. Sadly, Lee wasn't that old to be in such difficult shape. We learned that he was given away as a little boy and had never been a part of a "normal" family Christmas, so we included him in ours for a few years. Lee was like a child in his emotional development and we loved him. When my son Joseph was in high school he was assigned by me to help Lee. The job description included getting him to the bathroom and attending to any post-bathroom clean-up issues that might result. Needless to say, it wasn't a pleasant experience for Joseph. I told him it was character building, though in hindsight it might not have been all that much. But Joseph Phillips will never forget it, nor will my other children. It reminded all of them of the enormous blessings God has bestowed on us. They couldn't imagine not enjoying each other's company on Christmas. Lee couldn't imagine how wonderful Christmas could be. We tried to give him that. The Bible says, *"God sets the lonely in families..."* (Psalm

68:6, NIV).

One of our treasured holiday photos includes a teenager named Paul. We brought him into our home to spend Christmas with us one year. He came from circumstances as dysfunctional, if not more so, than mine. That Christmas we all had matching robes, and the kids sat on the fireplace hearth for our Christmas photo. One of the kids sat on Paul's lap. He was fifteen years old and he had never known a Jesus-filled, joyful Christmas with two parents who loved each other. Fast forward twenty years. Paul Denson enjoyed Christmas with us again last year. He brings his own two girls by the house for visits on occasion.

My wife Cecilia has a heart as big as Texas. She has modeled mercy and giving to our kids. I realize the holidays are a time to primarily focus on the family, but in Exodus we're given the principle of sharing. The twelfth chapter of Exodus teaches us about the Passover. Interestingly, God's instructions included a provision for people who didn't have a lamb: they were to share with their neighbor. We know that Jesus is our Passover according to the New Testament. We want to share the Lamb with people, especially at Christmas. We don't do it every Christmas but we're open to it every year. We celebrated one year with Naomi, who was a single young woman from a wonderful family. Unfortunately, that wonderful family was thousands of miles away.

Cecilia's heart and values have trickled down to the kids. Lauren has a similar giving spirit. One Thanksgiving Lauren invited several international students from her university, UNCC, to our table. They were from India and were interested in being part of an American holiday. We gave them the full experience, which included a prayer of gratitude and thanksgiving. As we made a circle in the den the students were genuinely alarmed. They had never actually prayed to God. We assured them there was nothing to be alarmed about and invited them to close their eyes and relax. We held hands and thanked God for all the good God stuff in our lives and family, including our guests. One of the international students later told Lauren, "I felt an unusual peace when your dad prayed. I can't explain it. It was warmth like the sun." Isn't it amazing that some people on the earth don't "have a prayer?" They literally have never prayed.

Special Events

It's been on my bucket list for thirty years to take my wife to San Francisco, California. One of the universities I played basketball for had a road trip to Northern California and I fell in love with the beauty of the place. We were finally able to scratch that off my bucket list last month as we spent five nights in California. She never really got it—my desire for her to see it—until we were there. Now she does and we hope to go again together.

Another bucket-list item was to take her to New York to see a Broadway play. We attended the one most recommended by critics. We didn't particularly like the play but we loved our special trip. New York has been special to several members of the family. (Later I'll share how that city helped me navigate "the talk" with our kids.) For example, last year we looked at a university in Manhattan that my daughter had been accepted to and had as one of her possibilities. Another time, I was in New York on a day trip with our sons (connected with a ministry trip, of course) when I received a call from my stepmother that my father had fallen in a creek, broken some ribs and was in very bad shape. In fact that fall precipitated an early death for Dad at the age of sixty-three.

I have some other items on my bucket list that involve Europe, ski slopes, and the Caribbean. Those are unchecked as of this writing. Special trips are good because they give the family something to look forward to, and they provide cherished memories that will be talked about for years. There is an excitement, anticipation and a controlled chaos in preparing for the event.

When I was a child I had friends I spent the night with from time to time. There were four kids in the family, two boys and two girls like in our family. The dad was a co-worker of my dad in the insurance business. Since I was an only child their family dynamic was like a sociology case study in chaos. They were Christians, and I remember two things about the time I spent with them. Number one, they carved soap, a relatively inexpensive hobby, somewhat dangerous but fun. Number two, they had a jug on top of the refrigerator that said, "Disneyworld or Bust," in which they collected change. Unfortunately, that trip was a "bust" for their family. They never went. I've often thought of that jug with sadness. Years later, I learned the father had taken his life in a spiral of depression. I often wondered if they had taken that trip to Disneyworld, or perhaps other trips that would have been fun for the family, if things would have been better. Maybe not. But the point I'd like to make is don't just dream about special trips. Don't say, "One day we'll do such and such." Plan for it. Do it. Even if the dream is modest. The Bible says, *"All hard work brings a profit, but mere talk leads only to poverty"* (Proverbs 14:23, NIV).

CHAPTER 2

HAPPY MARRIAGE, HAPPY FAMILY; HAPPY WIFE, HAPPY LIFE

Jerry

The Special Parts of Marriage

In every marriage there are special secrets, code words, looks, things you do for one another or an expression that tells it all—and only the couple knows this secret code. How you hold hands, how you embrace one another, speaks volumes of the special signs and expressions of love that have developed between the two of you. I know there are certain memories Libby and I can bring up that bring a smile to both of our faces.

Showing affection in front of others, including your children, is an interesting topic. Some live with the motto that you never show affection publicly, and these are the ones who, at the first sign of public affection, say, "Take it to the bedroom." The way you greet your mate or family when you come home from a trip or from work sends a message that your mate reads, your children see, and others observe.

Do you commemorate birthdays and anniversaries by doing something special for your spouse? Do you ever bring flowers for no other reason than to let your wife know you love her? Kids notice, kids *notice*—and did I say KIDS NOTICE these kinds of behaviors? They do! We need to let our children know we love one another and that it's okay to show some affection publicly. The facial expressions say it all when your mate stops by for lunch or you see them come in from a hard day's work. Your family notices the genuine expressions of love that you show.

I'll never forget one time when Libby and I stopped at the drug store so she could pick up a prescription. I stayed in the car with the kids, but as she walked into the pharmacy I said to the kids, "Your mother is a fox." Dustin, who was four years old at the time, quickly said, "She's not a fox!" I tried to explain that what I was saying was a compliment, that I thought she was hot. I wanted them to know I thought their mom was pretty. But it didn't register with Dustin or the girls. When Libby came back to the car Dustin told on me by saying, "Momma, Daddy called you a wolf." I laughed so hard while trying to explain to my wife that I had not called her a wolf, but I had called her a fox. So, from time to time, I tell Libby she's a wolf in memory of that funny moment. It's one of those private jokes that couples share.

Listen, I get it, our work is important, but there is nothing more important than our mates and our families. There will always be more meetings, more to-do's than you'll ever get done, so hear me: Focus on your family. Focus on what really matters in life more than self-serving focuses.

When you come home and she knows you've had a difficult day and greets you warmly, when she tells you to get into some casual clothes and that dinner will be ready soon, it feels great, it feels like she understands and cares, and it truly communicates her love for you.

Now, this works both ways. Do you do the same for her when you walk through the door? Do you notice the look on her face that says she feels all she's done all day is talk to kids, wash clothes and clean the house? Do you notice the look that says, "Please slow down and acknowledge that my motherhood matters?" Are you self-centered at that moment, or are you willing to lay aside your needs and be there for her? Do you ever say, "Honey, sit down and let me make dinner. Let me wash the dishes and you just sit down. I'll tuck the kids in tonight and you go take a long bath and I'll come rub your feet when I get the kids in bed." Okay, rubbing her feet may be taking it a bit far, but you get the idea. We men have to not be so selfish and self-centered when we come through the door at night. We must read the setting and make decisions that will bless our wives and our families. If you have a daughter, I know she will notice how Dad takes care of Mom when she needs a break. Your son will notice too.

And for those couples who both work and both come home from a busy day at the office, pulling a meal together and getting the kids managed is especially challenging. The workload for laundry, housecleaning, buying groceries, picking up the kids must be tasks that are fairly shared. It's too much for any one person to work a 40 or 50 hour week and then take on all of the challenges of the home.

These are the defining moments for enriching your marriage or for watching your marriage come apart. It's important that we really evaluate what it takes to run a home and make good decisions that will contribute to a healthy home environment. We as men must learn how to read these moments and do our best to respond appropriately. This is truly a learned behavior in men.

Your life together is about building memories, good ones … and some not so good. I remember one of our vacations that we were so excited about. We were going to Cape Cod to enjoy a week at the beach. We were picturing an amazing experience and couldn't wait to get there. Libby and I were coming off of a six-week, massive outreach in New York City, with over 300 workers we were responsible for. We had handled all the logistics for David Wilkerson to preach in the streets, following concerts by amazing bands we had recruited. We were both exhausted and truly needed our vision of a perfect vacation to be a reality.

But when we arrived in Provincetown, Massachusetts, on the tip of Cape Cod, our dreams were dashed. I won't go into all that we experienced. Suffice it to say it wasn't what we had dreamed of for our family vacation. There was some kind of conference or festival and the entire area was packed with people who were in a party mode. We had driven into a Sodom and Gomorrah-type atmosphere. The spirit of the event was overwhelmingly annoying. We left after one night and decided to drive the backcountry all the way to our home in Lindale, Texas.

We'd drive for a while then stop whenever something caught our attention. We browsed through antique shops, allowed the kids to swim all day while we lay beside the pool watching them enjoy themselves. One night we went to a drive-in theater, and our kids went right to sleep in their car seats as we watched the movie. It was quite nice for Libby and me. Though our "dream" vacation in Cape Cod was a bust, we had a really leisurely trip home and in the end it created a good memory.

Marriage brings many opportunities for mishaps. Each of us can likely remember at least one or two crazy things that happened to us at one time or another. One of those memories for me actually happened on the day I got married. About thirty minutes before my wedding I was leaving the hotel to go to the church, and as I bent down to get into my car my tuxedo pants split from belt loop to zipper. I was in instant panic mode, I had no idea how I would get my pants repaired in time for the wedding. I showed my best man what happened and he just laughed.

In my panic all I could think to do was get some safety pins, get to the church and repair the pants there. I confess my prayer life improved greatly as I prayed my pants would stay together for the ceremony. My biggest concern was that during communion I had to kneel down with my rear facing the crowd. I have never prayed so hard on a communion bench. I can tell you I moved in slow motion getting down on my knees, terrified of what might happen if the pins didn't hold. It was not one of the better memories of my wedding day.

Every couple has special ways they communicate, the bumps under the table, the looks that say it all. Those are parts of a relationship that need no explanation.

Recently, I told Libby I loved her and I wanted to grow old with her. I was thinking about the joy of spending the latter years of my life with the one I have loved for so long. I knew only she could truly appreciate all the memories we have built together, because those memories are only special between those who have experienced them together, whether they were good times or challenging times.

This is not to say that if you are in a second marriage you can't appreciate when your mate shares memories of their early years and enjoy them together. But there's something to be said for those who have spent thirty, forty or fifty years together in one marriage, building memories of a lifetime.

Libby and I will often text each other during the day and say something like, "Hey, I'm thinking of you! Love you!" or "I miss you already!" or "Love you, want to meet for lunch?" I often say, "Did I tell you yet today? Did I tell you I love you?" All I have to say now is, "Did I tell you today?" and she gets it.

When I am traveling I do my best to call her when I arrive at the hotel to let her know I'm safe and in my room. I want my wife to know I'm not out running around, doing something stupid. I don't want her to ever worry that she can't trust me when I travel, so I call her and we talk about our day or what we are expecting for tomorrow, or we talk about the kids.

Communication is very important when one of the mates travels.

I have to admit that other than special occasions I haven't been great at giving cards or flowers. As I write this I'm reminding myself that I should be better at this method of saying I love you to my sweet Libby. I just get in a rush and head home, still processing the activities and conversations of the day, and am mindless of such sweet opportunities to express my love and appreciation for her.

We need to do special things to show our loved ones that we're there for them, and remind them in special ways that they matter to us. This world and its technology are so distracting. We must lay the toys aside, spend time together, and listen to one other.

Libby and I have coffee together each morning I'm home, and when I'm away I'll often call her and ask if she has her coffee so we can have our time together. That's a special time each morning to pray together, to chat about what's happening over the next days, and what each of us has on our agendas. We talk and pray together about our family and life issues. I'm an early riser so I will have had my devotions by the time Libby comes in for coffee. But this has become a special time for us, a way to start our day together with "us" time. As I write this I'm mindful of how much I love Libby and how much this time together means to me, whether it's face to face or over the phone. Do you have "us" time with your mate? Let me suggest that you turn off the TV, or lay aside your computer or cell phone, and plan that time with your mate and loved ones.

Date Nights

Libby and I have not always practiced having consistent date nights and this is likely my fault. In fact is it my fault. We did have date nights for a while when the kids were young and we needed some alone time. I'd hire a babysitter one night a week and Libby and I would go out. It was a time in our lives when we had little money to do much, so we often went to parks and walked. I do remember many great conversations on park benches or just driving around together.

Libby and I love to look at real estate and love walking through model homes being built in our community. We enjoy seeing the new designs, architecture, layouts and furniture placement. Libby has such an eye for furniture placement and design. It doesn't cost anything and it's an enjoyable way to spend time together.

As our careers and our families mature we often face the challenge of balancing them. Our careers demand our time and commitment if they're going to succeed, and in many cases the survival of the business or ministry depends on us. At the same time, our mates and families are screaming for our attention. It truly is a tough balancing act for all of us.

From pre-school through high school our kids need us to be there for them. This is a critical time and it's important for us as parents to focus on them. There are times our children struggle with issues at school or church and they need some attention. We may not always know how to help them, but we can listen and lend our support and assure them of our love. That's a key way to be there for them. Our children have to walk through the challenges of life in order to grow into mature adults, and we need to be there to walk through those challenges with them.

But this can also be a time of pitfalls for our marriages, a time when our relationship with our spouse can falter. In the busyness of life and parenting we need to take time for our mates, to talk, to spend quality time together, and to attend to the pressures that surface at work and at home. Yes, these are critical years for us as parents, but they're also critical years for us as couples.

It's important for our kids to see us focus on our marriage and on one another. The way we treat our mate is critical to their well-being and sense of security. I remember kissing and hugging Libby in front of the kids and them laughing and teasing and giggling about it. They would see us kiss, embrace, or sit next to one another on the couch, and I truly believe it builds a deep sense of security in kids. They may say, "That's gross, stop it," but it really does mean a lot to them.

Commitments and Communication

When Libby and I got married, we made the commitment to never use the word divorce. We have been married for 39 years at the time of this writing and I cannot ever remember either one of us using the word divorce in any discussion. Have we had disagreements? Yes. Have we grown distant at times due to stress, distractions, and general life challenges? Yes. But, we work through those times and our relationship gets deeper and stronger as the years pass.

In our marriage, it seems Libby and I come to a place of transition every five years or so where we reach another level in our relationship. It's like we hit a hurdle that triggers a time of self-evaluation, and even frustration. There may be weeks or months of coolness or poor communication, but as we press through, we get to the next level and find our relationship is richer, and we find so much pleasure in one another's company. There is no scientific proof of this; I'm just telling you that life brings on new challenges at work, home and in relationships. Our experience has been that as we work together through the challenges, our marriage becomes deeper and richer.

We have some dear friends who made a pact with one another during the early and crazy years of raising three boys. They said that if one of them ever came to the place where they were thinking of divorce, the one who filed for divorce had to take the three boys. They laughed as they told us that, and you could see that after 40-plus years of marriage their commitment was still solid as a rock. Their boys are grown and have families of their own, but that little agreement was their way of saying, "We're committed to the end."

It takes work to navigate the pitfalls, and key to that is good communication. No matter how long you've been married, you have to communicate. The way you communicate may change over the years—we've certainly found that to be true—but it's important to respect one another and to allow each person the freedom to express their feelings. Libby and I can give one another a simple look and know exactly what the other person is feeling or thinking. I imagine the same is true for you. We know when our communication is off and we're getting a bit distant. We may ignore it for a few days, but then we address it and press forward. Marriage is hard work, but it is well worth the effort it takes to work through the challenges to reap the rewards of sharing life together.

A person could have a PhD in counseling and have taken many classes on the art of listening, and still need to learn more about effective listening. For the type-A, choleric personality who is running hard to accomplish their goals, the art of listening is a particular challenge. Make time to talk, to really communicate and listen to one another. Many times, the struggles that come in marriage are due to a breakdown in communication. Slow down and listen. Pay attention to the signs of stress, weariness and discouragement in your spouse and yourself before they get out of hand and destroy your marriage.

We all have times when we need someone to just listen to us without necessarily trying to fix the problem. And guys, let me say, I'm mostly talking to you. It's in our nature to want to fix things, but in most cases your wife just wants to be heard. I'm telling you this because this is really hard for me. I solve problems all day long and want to apply those same problem-solving skills to Libby and my children.

Listening requires that you turn your cell phone off or at least silence it. You know you can't listen and watch a game or worse, play a game. You do know that, right? I have been told that many times. The idea that one can multi-task and listen at the same time is a false concept. The moment my eyes slip away or I get that deer-in-the-headlights look, I get found out. I may be hearing, but I'm not listening.

I have tried writing emails and sometimes cards to express my love, my feelings, and sometimes my concerns. It seems to be deeply appreciated, more for the effort than for the quality of the communication.

Remembering birthdays and anniversaries is one of the ways to communicate that your mate is important to you. Those special dates are on my calendar and I've set them as annual events to help me remember. I do well at times and fail miserably at other times. I try to stop by a card shop and get a mushy card if I can. I actually like funny cards but they don't always express the love and admiration I have for Libby.

We have never made it a tradition on birthdays or anniversaries to go to a particular restaurant for dinner or a special B&B for a getaway, as some couples do, but as I write this, I wish we had. From this day forward I would love to take Libby some place special on our anniversary each year that becomes "our" place. I'd like to hear some of your traditions to help me with ideas.

Libby and I are truly enjoying this phase of life. Yes, our jobs keep us crazy busy, and, yes, we have three kids, their mates and our grandkids to attend to, but life in Christ is a journey. That journey has pain, suffering, and confusion at times, but it also brings overwhelming blessing and joy.

Joe

The Special Parts of Marriage

I knew I had married well during our first autumn as a couple. I was on the patio of our small apartment on a Saturday, reading or preparing a lesson, when I heard a scream come from inside. I flew into the apartment to find out what was wrong only to be greeted by my wife's embarrassed face and a sincere apology. "Honey, I'm sorry. Georgia just kicked a go-ahead field goal." Not only was she cheering for our favorite college football conference, the Southeastern Conference, but she was doing it alone. She didn't have to fake being a sports fan. Raised by a Hall-of-Fame sports broadcaster, she had and has a genuine appreciation for athletics. That may not be special to the reader but I assure you it is special to this writer.

"Special" means walking with your mate and discovering their likes and dislikes—stumbling upon the thing that makes them tick. There is an evolution. I have always liked sports. I have evolved in my appreciation for other things as well. For instance, years ago I couldn't tolerate HGTV. Now I watch it with Cecilia and sometimes I even enjoy it. I have begun to take an interest in cooking as well. Sharing is the name of the game. Sharing life, not just duties. Walking together is spectacular. Last week my wife was shocked that I could do a tedious crafty thing for our first grandchild's baby shower and that I could do it as well as she could. It was some type of little party favor. Wonders in marriage do not have to cease.

Date Nights

I contend that whatever won the affection of a mate needs to continue through the duration of that marriage. Dating, kindness to one another, taking care of one's personal appearance, sharing affection, etcetera, should continue. Dating each other with a child that arrived before our second anniversary was no easy feat, but in some ways it was more important than it had been when it was easy. We needed to carve out time for each other, for me to show Cecilia that she was important to me, and vice versa. The budget didn't allow for extravagant dates. Jerry already alluded to that. I look at dating on a shoestring in much the same way I look at Teen Challenge, especially juvenile Teen Challenge. I always say, "If you have a child on drugs you probably can't afford Juvenile Teen Challenge. But if it is your child, you can't afford NOT to get them into Teen Challenge." Even if you can't afford dating *per se*, you can't afford NOT to carve out special time for your spouse.

My friend, Pastor John Wood in Macon, GA, has done some comedy events with us and he has a bit regarding vacations and outings at different stages in life. It's hilarious when he does it. He says when you're young you ask, "Where did you go on vacation?" The answers are exciting and light up the speaker and the listener. "We went bungee jumping. Scuba diving. Cliff diving. Snorkeling. Skiing. Backpacking." Stuff like that. When you get old the conversation changes. "What did you do on vacation?" "We took a nap." The listener leans in and says, "Tell me about it. Don't leave out any details. Did you turn the attic fan on? What thread count were the sheets? Did you have a white noise machine? How long did you nap?"

I have discovered date nights are a bit that way. "Want to go downtown to a fancy restaurant? Want to go to a production?" Not so much. We're usually content to grab some take-out and go home and watch one of those Friday night news magazines on T.V., sitting beside each other on the couch. Just being together is what matters. Holding hands, deferring one to another, serving one another.

Commitments and Communication

On the California trip I referenced earlier I was honored to officiate at the wedding ceremony of a friend and former world champion wrestler. He and his bride wrote their own vows. One of the vows really struck me and stuck in my spirit. My friend said, "I vow to always protect your heart." Not just to provide for and physically protect his wife, but to literally protect her *heart*, the center of emotions. I made a commitment in that moment to do the same thing for my wife. I've thought about that every day since. It's a special commitment in marriage, to commit not to lose that tender tone of affection, not to lose the kindness and sweetness. I want to protect Cecilia's heart. Even if I must exercise God-ordained leadership in the home and fulfill that priestly office, I want to protect her in the process.

Another commitment I've made regarding Cecilia is to pray for her. I have freshly committed to pray *with* her. I was speaking at a minister's conference a few years ago and had some time at the end for questions and answers. A question came from an honest soul who asked, "Why is it so hard for me to pray with my wife?" My answer was, "Because she knows you, Turbo." All joking aside, he's right, it is hard, but that doesn't mean we shouldn't do it. Here's a good way to start. Rather than pray lengthy prayers for everything you can think of, including the county coroner and every missionary you've ever known, take your mate's hand and pray the Lord's Prayer from Matthew, chapter six. Dr. Mark Rutland wrote a book called *21 Seconds a Day to Change Your Life*. It's a profound little book that I recommend. It only takes twenty-one seconds to pray the Lord's Prayer, yet it can connect marriage partners and anchor them to something profound.

In *The Third Chair*, I wrote about the power of declaration. A decade ago I established a habit of saying ten things at the end of my prayer time with the Lord. I refer to them and journal them as "The Ten." One of the ten is: "My marriage is fruitful and prosperous like a fruitful vine." I don't believe there's a magic formula in that statement, but when I declare that over the course of years, where there is discord or strife—and every relationship hits bumps—I immediately, inherently, intuitively and instinctively know that the strife goes against the grain of what I have believed God for. The harsh word or attitude shows up in my spirit like a filthy hog at a gorgeous banquet. It doesn't belong and I work hard and quickly to escort it out. That commitment has been valuable to my marriage.

In 1992, Reverend Gary Chapman wrote a book called *The Five Love Languages.* He served as the senior associate pastor at Calvary Baptist Church in Winston-Salem, NC, at the time the book was published. It has been translated into forty-nine languages and has sold more than eight million copies. It is consistently in the top five on the New York Times Best Sellers' List. Gary Chapman struck a deep chord of truth with that book. He outlined five basic ways that men and women relate to each other and express and receive love: words of affirmation, physical touch, acts of service, gifts, quality time. I wish I had known those truths at the beginning of our marriage, because those principles work.

My primary love languages are physical touch and words of affirmation. I joke that one hundred people could say to me after I preach a sermon, "Joe that message changed my life. In fact, at our house we measure time by 'pre-Joe sermon' and 'post-Joe sermon.'" One hundred people could say that to me, but if my dear wife Cecilia said, "You know, Joe, that sermon wasn't half bad. In fact, it was pretty good," those words would trump all others by far. Her words are life to me. Sometimes I dwell on something she's said for weeks. When she holds my hand, brushes my shoulder or hugs me, I know she loves me. When I give her a smooch goodbye, I often have an involuntary physiological shudder. Literally I get a chill. She laughs and I get aggravated.

I don't want her to have the satisfaction of knowing the power she has over me. I say that in jest—mostly.

Because her words are so crucial to me, I mistakenly think she receives love in the same way. But that's not the case. Yes, she appreciates it when I say something nice to her but she doesn't live on the words like I do. Her love languages are different, and that challenges me. One of her love languages is gifts. She loves to receive and give gifts. I happen to receive gifts awkwardly. When she buys me a shirt thinking how much I'll love it, it just feels like an assignment to me. *Do I have to try it on and model it for her now? Do I have to give up a shirt I like to make room in my closet for this one? Which shirt do I wear the least? I hope she didn't spend too much on this.* My wife has what's been described by ladies as a "shopping anointing," meaning she has a gift for finding great deals. The point is I have to learn to communicate her love language. "What a nice shirt, Cecilia! Let me try it on immediately! Does it look good on me? Do you like it?"

I learned years ago that my wife isn't impressed by much, but if I want to get her attention and express love in a way she understands, connects with and responds to, I know just how to do it now. If she's been out, an hour or two before she comes home I'll jump in and do laundry or clean the house like a crazy man. When she walks in and sees my rear end sticking out of the refrigerator with two shelves of food on the counter, her heart flutters. It doesn't flutter at my blue-jeaned bottom. It flutters that I'm taking time out of my schedule to clean out the fridge. As the old song goes, "Get your motor running, head out on the highway, looking for adventure..." Acts of service. That's the other language she responds to. Jesus didn't come to be served, but to serve. We are created in His image. We are to love our wives like He loved the church. He served with a towel and a basin. So my rear end sticking out of a fridge, or me standing over a mop bucket, or my hand on a vacuum cleaner is actually quite Biblical.

There is a rhythm in communication. As we minister together, I may lead in prayer for someone at an altar, somewhere in America. When I'm finished praying I never have to ask my wife to pray. I simply touch the back of her hand or squeeze it if we're holding hands with the saint. Without missing a beat she'll continue the prayer. It's a rhythm, a means of communication we've developed in our years of marriage. You learn each other. The Bible says to dwell with your wife according to knowledge. Men, we need to *know* our wives. When does she need my shoulder and not my mouth? When does she need to be heard and not advised (probably most of the time)? My wife has type 1 diabetes. Cecilia's blood sugar predicates the level of communication. If she is low, I *know* it's not a good time to ask her for advice for a decision I'm trying to make. When I *know* it's high, I tell myself not to be offended if she isn't warm and fuzzy. How can I *know* something as specific as blood sugar? There's a look on her face. Communication is about knowing and timing.

I have a comedy bit that goes briefly like this. Men are like dogs. Dogs are predictable. I can go outside and get something out of my truck and when I return in two minutes my dog has the same reaction as if I'd been gone for two days. Scratch a dog behind the ear, feed it meat and let it run in the yard and basically you understand the nuances of a dog. Women are like cats. "You may pet me if you must. I am going under the couch now. I'll see you in two days. I am not eating that food. Don't move it! I might eat it tomorrow." You can put a dog on a leash, but not a cat. I tried once in my adulthood, which bespeaks of my IQ, common sense, or lack of both. It seems women want men to be mind-readers. Men are not good at that, like, at all! So, ladies, please communicate directly with thick-skulled men like me. Instead of saying, "It's weird that, lately, the trash seems to get full faster,"—which may only garner a manly grunt—say something like, "Honey, would you mind taking out the trash?" The best line of communication at my house would be, "Baby, you are so great about this. I hate to ask, but would you take out this trash again?" Absolutely! We joke that years ago my wife would ask, "Do you even know me?" Or she might simply declare, "You don't know me at all!" Finally, one day I answered, "Apparently I don't, but I'm trying!" Let's keep trying, boys.

CHAPTER 3

BOUNDARIES:
MINISTRY, BUSINESS AND FAMILY

Jerry

Travel

Do you travel in your ministry or business? My career has had me traveling most of my married life. Early on in my work with David Wilkerson Crusades, I set ground rules for myself to protect me when I traveled. For instance, I have a rule that when I get to the hotel room for the night, I stay there. I don't go out to check out the community. I always eat in restaurants and not in hotel bars. I don't go into the bar at night for a snack. I'm careful with the TV stations I watch in hotel rooms. I do my best to never be away from home more than ten days at a time unless Libby is with me. I always let her know where I'm staying, and I call home to talk to her and the kids often. I have no secrets when I'm traveling. If you travel for your job, you too must set boundaries or you will face temptations of every variety.

Another ground rule to set is that you keep all your receipts and are accountable for how you spend company or ministry money while you travel. This is critical, as it reflects on you personally. You need to be disciplined in this for your own protection and for the trustworthiness that is built between you and those to whom you are accountable.

When my kids were young, and also during their teen years, I made it a point to be home by Friday night at 5 p.m. so we could spend the weekend together. It wasn't always possible, but those weekends when I was home were totally focused on my wife and kids. Yes, we did chores and necessary shopping, but I made sure my family knew I wanted to spend time with them, no matter what we did. We let them help decide what movies we watched, what games we played, and we even let them have friends over to join in the fun. I have no doubt that my children have fond memories of those days.

One of the things that I didn't recognize was the changing role Libby experienced every time I left for a trip. When I was home, she would defer authority to me. We would work together on decisions regarding the kids, finances and family. Then I would leave for a trip and Libby would instantly become the authority. She took control of decisions while I was away, though we sometimes consulted about issues by phone when necessary. Then she took a step back and let me be in charge again when I came home. I never realized how difficult that might be for her, mostly because she was so gracious about it. One day long after the kids were out of the house she brought it up and I was surprised by the discussion. I felt bad that I had not recognized how hard that had been for her and how I should have recognized and acknowledged her effort. So, if you travel a great deal for work or ministry, acknowledge this and give your mate some praise for their effort in managing this changing role.

When our kids were growing up, playing board games was one of their favorite activities. When their friends came over, they would ask them if they wanted to play games. Sometimes their friends were surprised by that, but once they played games all night, laughed and had a blast, they wanted to come over again and again to play. Even when our kids came home from college they would ask to play board games. Their college friends gave them strange looks, but when game night was over, they had really enjoyed themselves. Some of their friends would even ask to come over and play when my kids weren't in town. What a fun family tradition.

Cell Phones

Cell phones continue to dominate people's lives. I have had a cell phone since they came out with a carry bag phone. Over the years I've made a few rules on cell phone use. When my kids were still living at home, I made it a practice to turn the phone off before entering the house. If I was on a call when I got home, I'd finish the call before going inside, then the phone was off at least until the kids went to bed. I didn't want my cell phone ringing when I came through the doors so I could focus on my wife and kids for the evening. I would turn it back on about 9 p.m. to keep up with anything that was critical. Even now that our children are grown and no longer living at home, when I pull up in my driveway I finish any call I may be on before going inside, because my time with Libby is just as important to me. I may leave my phone on these days, but I still want to focus on my wife and any guest that may be with us when I'm at home. I'm also very restrictive on the weekends as to how much I'm on my phone. I've had enough of it during the week and I figure most emails can wait a few days. I have an executive assistant who reviews emails for me occasionally on weekends, and if something is critical she will text or call me if something is time sensitive.

I know that just hit some of you right between the eyes, and those of you who are married have likely had several fights over this one issue. Our cell phones should not dominate our time off. Let me repeat that, our cell phones should not dominate our time off. They have off switches, for meals, for special times together with your family, etcetera, turn them off.

My kids all have cell phones and bring them with them when they visit. We have cell phone chargers everywhere. We're all trying to decide whose phone is whose. I have finally decided to make everyone turn off their phones during dinner time and not turn them on again until we've had dessert and finished visiting. I ask that they don't even have them on vibrate so we don't have to think about whose phone is buzzing.

I once shared a room with someone who was truly addicted to his cell phone. He slept on his back with his phone on his chest. He liked to take long hot baths and would carry it into the bathroom with him and I would hear him on it while he was in the tub. He was also a micro-manager, which meant his phone rang all the time. He made every little decision about every issue in his organization. On one call he decided the color of the trash can in the women's bathroom. That's when I spoke up and challenged him on his phone use and his need for affirmation via the phone, as if his worth was determined by the number of times his phone rang and the amount of time he spent on it. If this hits home, may I suggest you turn your phone off now and then and learn to control it rather than allowing it to control you. Wives, you can thank me by buying another one of these books for other men you know who are addicted to their cell phones.

Respect

As parents, we felt it was critical that each member of our family respected one another. We wanted them to love and appreciate each other's differences as well as their individual gifts and contributions to the family. We taught our kids the importance of respecting the authorities over them and to respect others, especially older adults.

We wanted our kids to learn to respect one another's things as well. If they wanted to borrow something from someone in the house, they had to ask permission to use it, and then they had to put it back where they got it. We expected them to take care of what they borrowed, and to be considerate when their brother or sister wanted to borrow something from them.

Yes, sir; no, sir; yes, ma'am; no, ma'am were words we taught our kids to use. We modeled that by using those words ourselves when we spoke to older adults in our lives.

One day I came in quietly through the front door and overheard my son speaking to my wife in a disrespectful way. He was 15 at the time and playing football at school. It seemed some testosterone had gotten up between his ears. He and his mom were in the kitchen and didn't know I was in the house, overhearing the way he was talking to his mother. As I came around the corner of the living room and he saw me, his face registered his shock. I stopped, looked into his eyes and said, "Son, you will not speak to your mother like that, and you will not speak to my wife like that." He was quiet a moment and then he said, "You know, Dad, I can take you."

That was the testosterone speaking, and it brought out a side of me that didn't often surface. I walked around the kitchen counter and squared off in front of him. I will refrain from sharing with you all that I said to my son, but he was sent to his room without dinner, until he could come and apologize to his mother. It was a few hours before he came out of his room and approached Libby. He said, "I'm sorry, Mom, that I was disrespectful, and, Dad, I'm sorry I spoke to Mom that way. I got to thinking about what you said. I wouldn't want anyone speaking to my future wife like that and I get it. I'm sorry." We never had another real issue with him being disrespectful to his mom. I thank the Lord that our kids mature and see the value of treating one another with respect.

The Value of Getting Away

I learned a long time ago how important it is for Libby and me to get away for some quality time alone. One way we do that is to take *islands* of time together. I learned this concept from Dr. James Dobson when I heard him speak on his radio show about how he and his wife would schedule *islands* of time during the year to get away and get rejuvenated. At the first of each year they would sit down with their calendars and schedule weekend trips together, and he was not allowed to book anything over those dates. Typically, they would leave on a Thursday afternoon and come back on a Sunday night or Monday morning. This would give them enough time to get rested and break the routine of work, as well as see a few things they might want to see. Libby and I have borrowed this idea from the Dobson's, and do our best to get away for a few days, from time to time, to be alone together and rest. It is critical to maintain balance in our lives over the long haul of life, and this is one way to do that.

I also mentioned in Chapter 1 that taking two weeks at a time for vacation is critical to getting the kind of rest I need. I suspect you need it too, and I don't apologize for mentioning it again, especially for those of you who feel your business or ministry won't make it without you if you're away for that amount of time. And if it won't, you haven't learned to delegate. You may also have a control problem. Let it go. Trust people and let them lead. You may be pleasantly surprised and you'll get much more meaningful rest. You may even become a nicer person to be around. You can thank me when you see me, and you can buy another book for someone else who needs to read this.

Your Kids in Your Ministry

I was asked recently if I made my kids get involved with my Teen Challenge ministry. It was a joy to share with them how Libby and I had worked with our kids during their early years. I traveled on many Sundays of the year, speaking and having one of our Teen Challenge choirs join me. We wanted our kids to have a home-church experience so Libby stayed home with our children most Sundays unless I decided to take the whole family to a service with me. As they got a little older, I began to invite one child at a time to join me for the weekend, which they thought was great. So one of my three children would join me when I traveled for a service over the weekend. In the beginning we would hop in the van with the Teen Challenge choir and we would all go together. Then I decided I wanted the travel time alone with my children, because it was great one-on-one time, where we could talk, laugh, listen to music, and be in church together. As my kids got older they would ask questions like, "How far is this trip today? Do we have services at night as well? When will we get home?" Then they would decide if they wanted to go or not. Sometimes they all decided they wanted to be at our home church with their friends and I'd go alone, but usually one of them would go with me.

Let me take a moment to caution you parents who take your children to work or places of ministry with you. Be sure you keep a close eye on them, and be mindful of who they are with during the hours you are working. Don't leave them to entertain themselves or entrust them to people you aren't absolutely trustful of. I say this because two different friends of mine shared with me that their children had been molested while left in the care of staff/ministry team members. They believed they could trust their employees/ministry partners, but when they eventually learned the truth and heard their children talk about the pain they carried because of those experiences, they were heartbroken and guilt-ridden. Do everything you can to safeguard your children so they don't become statistics. If you take them to work with you or places of ministry in order to spend time with them, don't pass them off to others, but really spend the time together. I know this can be challenging, but listen to me, your kids deserve your watchful eye and protection more than ever before. When you consider how many people are struggling with pornography addictions, this should let you know that you can never be too careful. Don't live in fear, but don't be naïve either. If you have young children and use babysitters, make good decisions about who looks after them.

We never pressured our kids to work for Teen Challenge, but over the years each one of them has been an employee of ours. At the writing of this book, my oldest daughter Denee' and her husband Alan are becoming world missionaries and will work with Global Teen Challenge. My middle daughter, Kristi, and her husband, Ben, are pastors, and my son, Dustin, and his wife, Janel, are directors of our Teen Challenge Emerging Leaders College. It is encouraging that all three are in ministry, and it indicates to me that they were well-adjusted as the children of parents in ministry with really busy schedules. I believe it's because my children knew that though I worked hard, when I was home, I was home for them and work was set aside. It's tough to balance it all, but I know God will help you as he has helped us.

I want to say that Libby is the true hero for taking on so much of the home responsibilities as I had to travel so much through the years. She is a special lady and it is to her praise that our kids are as well-balanced as they are.

Joe

Travel

Billy Graham changed the world. I recently went with a pastor friend as he spoke at the daily devotional session for the employees of the Billy Graham Evangelistic Association. There were hundreds of employees there. I was honored to be given a tour of the facility by the administrative assistant for the legendary singer Cliff Barrows. There were too many impressive things to see, experience and process to articulate here. One thing that was very evident was the transparency. Every office, including Reverend Graham's, had ceiling-to-floor glass windows. I was told that it was a direct result of the Modesto Manifesto. Billy Graham was thirty-one years old in 1948. He was coming off a successful run as the evangelist for Youth for Christ. He was about to embark on a sixty-year career as an evangelist. His revival team included George Beverly Shea, Grady Wilson, and Mr. Barrows. The quartet was young and charismatic. Temptations abounded then as they do today. To guard themselves against allegations and to guard against the actual abuse of sex, power and money that had ruined previous ministries, the Billy Graham team decided to take concrete steps to avoid even the smallest hint of controversy.

The team gathered in a hotel room in Modesto, California. They formulated an agreement that became known as the "Modesto Manifesto," though they produced no written document. The manifesto included provisions for distributing money raised by offerings, avoiding criticism of local churches, working only with churches that supported cooperative evangelism, and using official estimates of crowd sizes to avoid exaggeration. The most famous provision of the manifesto called for each man on the Graham team never to be alone with a woman other than his wife. Graham, from that day forward, pledged not to eat, travel, or meet with a woman other than Ruth, unless other people were present. This pledge enabled Billy to avoid accusations that ruined other evangelists.

I am an evangelist who has always been impressed by Dr. Graham. I have no manifesto but I do have policies regarding travel. It's a different day and a different economy. I sometimes have a team with me, but many times I travel alone. Almost without exception when I go to a hotel, I take a picture of the hotel phone. I text it to each member of my family by group text. I include the phone number. I turn off my phone at night to rest deeply and avoid all the pings and dings that technology serves up. However, I want to be accessible to each person in my family. If my hotel phone rings in the night, I know it's going to be something serious. That policy serves as a comfort to me. I believe it's comforting to the family as well.

I have policies for the remote control as well. I went on a stint of two years without touching a remote control while traveling. The television was a colossal distraction, and filthy programming didn't have to be searched for. It was and is plentiful. One year at a hotel in Virginia, the Master's Golf Tournament ended my long streak. I probably need to implement the policy again. Policies and boundaries serve marriages and families well.

Another policy I have regarding travel is about my suitcase. I unpack my suitcase ninety-nine percent of the time as soon as I get home and put the suitcase in the closet. If I arrive home late, I'll do it first thing the next morning so as to not awaken Cecilia. That's my policy even if I'm home only a day or two. Early on, I made a decision that I didn't want my children to remember, even in a subliminal way, that Dad lived out of a suitcase.

Jerry has a lot of great stories about traveling all over the world. I have my fair share as well. One that comes to mind is from the Appalachian Mountains of Virginia. I held a revival in a little village where there wasn't a hotel or motel within fifty miles. Fifty miles in the Virginia and West Virginia mountains aren't like fifty miles in South Georgia. It may take two hours and ten minutes one way to travel those miles. This particular church had a repurposed Sunday school room they used as a "prophet's chamber," or evangelist's quarters. The village and church building were old by American standards. That big two-story, brick building groaned with the wind. There was plenty of wind. Now, your courage may be greater than mine. I have to admit that the church building spooked me. When an insomniac squirrel jumped on the gutter, or maybe it was a tree branch than fell at 2 a.m. on that particular windy night, it made a sound. The sound in my imagination was what unleashed demons on pigs might sound like. Travel has unique experiences, joys and obstacles.

Respect and Cell Phones

Jerry and I line up closely on the concept of respect, of course. It's a family value. We discuss values later. I was born "up north" but call myself a converted Southerner. I embraced early on saying "yes, sir" and "no, sir." It was and is a sign of respect. During a three-year ministry stint in Ohio, Cecilia and I learned that concept wasn't shared by the public school officials where our children went to school. They viewed "yes, sir" and "no, sir" as a sign of *dis*respect. We were floored when written reprimands came home saying the kids were disrespecting teachers by saying, "yes, ma'am."

Cell phones are wonderful tools that enhance our lives as well as aggravate the life out of us. I am not good at establishing some boundaries. We try to enjoy some activities that would not be pleasant with phones in our hands.

I may not add any good information here but I will throw in a comedy bit about social media found on so-called smart phones. Have you tried to put down the phone lately? I told my kids on a vacation that "Daddy is going to put his phone down for a week." I made it until Wednesday. By Wednesday I felt like I needed to download a Teen Challenge application. I felt like an addict. My teeth started itching, my hair started twitching and my eyes watered. I wanted to call a middle school kid and say, "Meet me at the 7-11. I'm paying good money for notifications. Extra cash for direct messages. Do you have a couple of tweets you can throw in for good measure?" Pitiful.

Cell phone boundaries are a challenge. Sometimes we all agree on putting them down. Sometimes we are in the same room but never together, as everyone has a device in hand. The Holy Spirit helps us with these types of issues and they can be more fluid than other issues and situations.

The Value of Getting Away: How Do You Spend Time Together?

When I'm not traveling we begin our day the way most of humanity begins theirs: waking up in a bed. Almost every day Cecilia and I say to each other, "Good Morning, I love you." Jerry talks about "islands of time." I loved Jerry's idea of morning coffee prayers. I plan on implementing that. I pray the Lord's Prayer at least one time per day with Cecilia. That's a little island as well.

I heard a story about a man who took his son fishing. They fished all day and went home to their journals. The entries were vastly different. The boy wrote, "I went fishing with my dad today. It was the best day of my life." The father wrote, "Went fishing. Got nothing accomplished. Wasted the whole day."

I make one-on-one time to get away with each of the kids as often as possible. That time is never a waste. It may be just a couple of hours in a coffee shop. It might be a hike in the woods. Those carved-out islands of time are truly wonderful.

Your Kids in Your Ministry

My kids have been around the family business their whole lives. Here is a brief inventory of all the Phillips' moves. We have done ministry in Fort Lauderdale, FL (twice); Columbus, GA; Concord, NC (twice); Atlanta, GA; Macon, GA; and Huntington, WV. That list represents a great deal of change. We've lived in fourteen dwellings, the kids have gone to an untold number of schools, they've had countless friends, have had numerous cultural mores to learn and all the other things that go with that kind of childhood. We moved almost as much as military families.

There are some great things about that kind of lifestyle. One, the kids always had a built-in support system: they became each other's best friends, especially when friends were in short supply or the friend pool to draw from was brand new. Second, they broadened their worldview. There is something to be said about roots and stability. It is to be valued. However, blowing all over the country gave the kids a buffer against an "I wonder what's out there" longing, because they had already been "out there." Another advantage is that they learned how to talk to adults because they were often in a position to have to deal only with adults when other kids were in short supply.

Much of life is about perception and vision. When I was a denominational leader in Georgia, we had PK (Preachers' Kids) retreats. We offered a free and fun weekend for all the interested parties in that huge state. I'll never forget one particular night around the campfire in the mountains. I told the preachers' kids it was a safe place to express how they felt about being the children of ministry. (They're all adults now with their own children so I break no confidences in this book.) One by one they spoke so poignantly and gut-wrenchingly about their feelings. "I hate it. The people are mean to my parents." "I hate seeing my parents cry." "Just when I make friends we have to move to some other town for a new church." "We don't make enough money to live on." I expected some of this, but not so much and not by everyone. I got to the end of the circle—mercifully!—and the last child, a thirteen-year-old girl, said something I haven't forgotten in fifteen years. Almost apologetically she said quietly and meekly, "I like being a preacher's kid. When the evangelist comes to town we get to eat steak." I know pain is real and church junk can be real junk. But I wanted to find the parents of that child and hug their necks, as we say down south. I knew the parents. They had been through some junk like the rest of us. Somehow they had helped their kids equate their life station with steak and positive experiences.

I believe joy is very important in any home. I recently sent out a tweet (if the reader sees these words in the future and doesn't understand "tweet," it was a platform for, well, never mind. Just google it). The tweet said, "Joyless households are weak households. Joy is strength. Put the family in the den. Turn up the dance music and get a little stronger." "...*for the joy of the Lord is your strength*" (Nehemiah 8:10). The Christian life, the Christian family life, is a paradoxical one. A paradox is "a statement or proposition that seems self-contradictory or absurd but in reality expresses a possible truth." Consider these paradoxical statements from Scripture: *"sorrowful, yet always rejoicing; poor, yet making many rich; having nothing, and yet possessing everything"* (2 Corinthians 6:10). There is a counterintuitive reality of being sorrowful and rejoicing at the same time. As leaders, parents model this reality to their children. "We are sad that people have been mean, but we are forgiven. We are going to heaven. We have the power of the Holy Spirit within us. There is a joy in laying nothing to the charge of the offenders and praying like Jesus taught us, '*as we forgive our debtors.*' Can you feel it, kids? Get in the den! We don't have much, but we have everything. We have Christ. Turn up the dance music!"

Church kids get a reputation—especially preachers' kids. I don't subscribe to the preconceived notions that certain humans are supposed to behave a certain way. Dr. Phil, the T.V. star, says, "The best indicator of future behavior is past performance." There is truth in that. I don't want to paint anybody into that corner or any other corner. I believe in the sovereign power of God to change things and situations. Just because thousands of preachers' kids have turned out as wild as bucks doesn't mean all preachers' kids or church kids have to turn out that way. I don't know how to preclude the manifestation of crazy in the life of a kid. I know better parents than myself whose children went through some very deep stuff. We simply tried to love our kids, tell them the truth and set a few boundaries. We also tried to make sure there was joy in the journey.

Cecilia and I are proud of our kids. They've all grown up with different gift sets, and different appetites and disciplines. We have done two tours of duty on the evangelistic field. The first one was from 1994 to 1995. Whew, it was *tough!* We went without a lot of things, but one great, bright spot was taking my little boy all over the Southeast with me. I did a lot of youth events back then and he loved being around teenagers. I wondered how he weathered some of those forty-five minute sermons, but I stopped wondering the night he told me, "Dad, you left out the dog story in point number two." He was six years old. Being a church kid or a PK didn't damage him in the least. In fact, it forged his future.

One of the happiest things about raising children is watching them learn to stand on their own two feet. It's what parenting is all about. As parents, Cecilia and I did our best and trusted God to do the rest. Our son Joseph is a preacher. Below is a blog post he wrote about being a preacher's kid. I use it with his permission. I'm biased, of course, but I think he's a brilliant writer and communicator.

I feel like a predictable anomaly. I am a pastor's kid who ended up being a pastor. Predictable, because isn't that what all pastors' kids end up doing? An anomaly, because after someone has been through everything ministry has to throw at them, why would anyone sign up for that?

One major reason I didn't run from what I feel God has called me to is my dad. On the whole, he didn't shield my eyes from the dark side of ministry. He didn't try to convince me that it was all beautiful and sentimental. He let me look fully at the rough edges of dealing with people. He didn't hide the reality of ministry from me but he did protect me from becoming bitter. He didn't respond in anger to injustices. He prayed for folks who persecuted him. He turned the other cheek when I didn't want him to. He showed me how to keep a pure heart when the circumstances could easily turn a heart to stone. He modeled what it means to be a pastor for me.

I've seen my dad preach to 10,000 people at one time in Brazil (the same trip he preached on a South American TV station to millions across the continent). I've seen him pray for the sick and see dramatic healings. I've seen countless people come to know Jesus through his ministry. But those aren't the things that stick out as extraordinary to me. I'm struck time and again by the fact that he still tears up talking about what Jesus has done in his life. I am awed when people from churches we were at fifteen years ago call my dad during crisis moments in their lives.

What he wrote touches my heart deeply.

CHAPTER 4

THE PARENTING EXPERIENCE

Jerry

Having Children

The day you get to take your first child home from the hospital is an amazing day. I will never forget getting out of the car at our home and holding Denee' as we walked into the house. I was ecstatic and terrified at the same time. I'll never forget that feeling of fatherhood and feeling the strong desire to care for and protect her, but I quickly realized I needed more training on how to do that. I experienced those same feelings with each of my children and now my grandchildren.

There were people in our lives who assured us that cloth diapers were best for newborns, so Libby and I decided that's what we would do if it was going to be better for our baby. But when I took that first cloth diaper to the toilet to rinse the "stuff" out of it, I began to question our decision. I was to dunk the diaper in the toilet and try to get the stuff to fall off into the toilet, then deposit that wet diaper into a plastic bin where other diapers were being stored in a blue-chemical liquid until laundry day. That was the same day we bought our first package of disposable diapers. I mean, how bad could they be if so many parents were using them? That was the end of cloth diapers in our house. Praise God! I know that if you have kids, you probably have some funny stories about diapers too.

Changing diapers is part of the job description of a father. Did you hear me, Dad? I know it's not one of the things you thought about as you considered marriage. But it comes with fatherhood and is a loving way to show your wife you are willing to help with raising your kids. One evening Libby asked me to change our daughter's diaper and I was only too happy to help. The next morning I was getting ready for work and Libby called to me from the baby's room. She said, "Jerry, did you change Kristi's diaper last night?" I said yes, then she asked, "Did you put the diaper in the trash?" "I think so," I replied. Then Libby said, "You may want to come see this." I walked into the nursery and got the shock of my life. Because I had, in fact, left the dirty diaper in the crib with Kristi, and she had "painted" the wall, every spindle on her bed and everything else within reach of her crib with that diaper's contents. The smell was awful, but the sight was nothing short of laughable. I don't know how she managed to get so much stuff on so many things, including covering herself from head to toe. But it was definitely my responsibility, so I picked her up, held her as far from me as my arms would stretch, and took her to the tub for a bath while Libby cleaned up the room. It was the worst mistake I had ever made with a diaper. Stop laughing, I mean it, stop laughing, because I know you've done something equally funny or stupid.

The first steps, the first words spoken, and the unique actions and expressions of each child all have a way of bringing so much joy to your life as a parent. But it can also be a stressful time for a young family. Our jobs get demanding, the kids have childhood illnesses that keep us home from work more often than we can afford, and teething or colic create sleepless nights for Mom and Dad. Let me encourage you, these days come and go quickly, so slow down and enjoy them.

As a couple you have to work on how to manage all the added responsibilities of having children. Libby and I shared many of the new tasks that came with having babies. She carried much of the load while I was at work, but I tried to help out in the evenings and on weekends with diaper duty, housecleaning, lawn maintenance and necessary home repairs. Raising kids is work, and there can be misguided assumptions that *going to work* is the *only* work. The days of the La-Z-Boy chair and the wife being the personal attendant are over. We own the responsibility to partner with our mates and invest in the shared responsibility of raising a family. If we can learn to love unconditionally and serve one another, we all win. Our mates win, we win and our family wins.

Now I have the joy of grandkids, and believe me, grandparenting brings so many wonderful experiences. I still change diapers from time to time, though I do my best to get out of that, even though I love my grandchildren dearly. Besides, their parents are responsible for diaper duty, right?

Communication

Listen, our kids need us to speak to them. I can't tell you how many times over the years I've appreciated the fact that my parents told me repeatedly that they loved me. I've tried to practice this throughout my parenting, so my children never doubted that I love them. Almost every day when they were living at home I would tell them I loved them. I still do, even though they're married and raising their own families. It never stops being important. I tell my wife I love her everyday as well.

Children don't understand the concept of quality time verses quantity of time. Quality time is a convenient concept for parents who need an excuse for their absenteeism, but what children understand is time. Children equate *quality* time with *quantity* of time, as well as the love and affirmation they receive. Children understand that words matter, time matters, and being there for them matters. We need to be at their school programs, their ball games, their piano recitals, or whatever else they're involved in. These times matter to them. Dads and moms can *never* delegate affection and their own child rearing responsibilities.

I heard a young lady whose parents were divorced speak of an uncle who visited her home often. He would tell her she was stupid and that she'd never amount to anything except being a whore. Those words crushed her spirit and her desire to excel in school or sports. They filled her mind with self-doubts and led to very poor self-esteem.

That's not at all surprising. I mean, who wouldn't feel bad about themselves with words like that being said to you, over and over? Her mom was not one to compliment or encourage either, which compounded the problem. The words drove this young lady to self-hate and self-destruction and became a self-fulfilling prophecy. She became exactly what she had been told she would become. Now, however, she has found freedom from addiction and is finding new life in Christ. She is being told, "You are new creation in Christ Jesus and old things have passed away. You have a future, and God has a plan for your life, "plans to prosper you and not to harm you, plans to give you hope and a future" (Jer 29:11, NIV), and those words are transforming her.

Our children need encouragement and affirmation, and if they don't get it from us, where will they get it? We need to feed our kids with hope, with love and encouragement about the purpose God has for their life. We need to encourage their dreams and help them excel in areas of their individual gifting. We set the tone for their life, so we need to affirm and encourage them, and challenge them to be all they can be in Christ.

Please don't miss the opportunity while your kids are still at home to say, "I love you, I'm proud of you, and you are special to me." Take time to listen to them, hear their thoughts, listen to them tell what their day was like. Their field trips, school events and daily issues are big to them. Just listen.

Chores and Responsibilities

We started our kids on chores at an early age. They were four or five years old when we began requiring them to clean their rooms before going to bed or going out to play. Libby was great at getting the children to follow through on their chores. She taught them to clean up one set of toys before getting another set of toys out. She had to remind them of that requirement more often than not, but it worked for the most part. And now she's teaching our grandchildren the same concept when they come to our home. Libby has shelves full of toys for the different age groups. She has projects for them, as well as coloring books, sticker books and other crafts to keep them busy doing things they enjoy. Even the two-year-olds know where the toys are and go right to the cabinets where they're kept, their eyes bright with excitement, when they come through the door.

As I said, the kids learned to clean their own rooms from a young age. They also helped in the kitchen with cooking and clean-up. As they got older they each had a night to do dishes and help in cleaning the house. They also helped me clean the car, mow the lawn and pick up leaves in the yard. They always helped clean up after birthday parties and holiday events. We wanted them to learn to be responsible with their things as well as how to maintain a home. They needed to learn that they were part of a family and that we each owned responsibilities within the family.

Our television was always off at mealtime, always. Did you hear me? *Always* off at mealtime. I hope by repeating myself you catch the importance of that and do the same. We set that rule early on in our marriage and we never allowed the television or our cell phones to disturb our precious time around the table together.

Please don't get me wrong. I don't mean to imply we were perfect parents. We weren't, and we wish we had done even more to encourage our kids regarding their talents and giftings. We can only pray we didn't keep them from being all they can be and utilizing the gifts God has endowed them with.

Effective Discipline for Pre-Teens

Libby had a remedy for our kids whenever they said, "I'm bored." She would say, "Okay, let me find something for you to do," and she would assign them a household task they had to complete before they could do something they wanted to do. That was a good solution to stop our kids from saying they were bored.

My dad did the same with my siblings and me. If we ever said we were bored, he would put us to work raking pine straw in our one-acre yard, which had one-hundred pine trees. They produced more pine straw than any trees on earth, at least that's what I thought as a teenager. I remember my dad saying to my sister as she raked that pine straw for what seemed like hours, "Are you still bored?" I learned to never say I was bored.

When it came to discipline for our kids, we used time-outs as one of our main tools to help correct their bad attitudes and behavior. It worked most of the time. Recently, one of my granddaughters was in a time-out and she was having a ball. Her mother went to see who she was talking to, and she proceeded to introduce her to the new best "friends" she had made while in time-out. Of course, these two new friends were imaginary. My granddaughter wanted to make sure her mother got their names right as she introduced them. My daughter couldn't stop laughing as she told us the story.

There were times we resorted to giving a few swats on the bottom, but only for the worst offenses. I had an old western belt I would use for swats, and just bringing it out of the closet got the immediate attention of the offender. My son was petrified of that belt. He knew he was in for it if Dad brought it out. We didn't have to do this very often, but it was effective in deterring unwanted behavior.

If you're thinking about calling the police on me for spanking my kids, get real. Kids need to know who's in charge and that better be the parent. If you make a little emperor or a queen out of your kids they will rule you and your household. The Bible says "spare the rod, spoil the child," and I believe that is absolutely true. I never beat my children, but a swat on the backside was generally a healthy way of getting their attention. It seemed to help them let go of bad behavior.

Most of the time we only had to sit them down and explain to them we weren't going to allow their disobedience. The kids generally got the point and settled down. Other times we had to take away privileges to get their attention. For example, they might not be able to go to a friend's house, or they might have to do extra chores if they were misbehaving. Those types of discipline worked very well with our children.

Fun Things We Did with Our Kids

Living in Florida, we spent most of our vacations at the beach when our kids were growing up. Libby and I still do. Our kids loved playing in the water and looking for shells. Usually we took a boat so we could go out to an island off the coast of Florida to find shells. On one trip we found over a hundred sand dollars which kept us entertained for hours. My kids had so much fun gathering shells and making special things with them. We made lamps and other decorative jars with the shells our kids found, and they loved doing that. It was a family activity that everyone enjoyed. We still have many of those pieces, and they spark great memories of family vacations for us and our grown kids.

When our kids were between the age of five and ten, we had what we called "Tent Night." This was usually on a Friday or Saturday night, and we allowed the kids to build a tent anywhere in the house, except our bedroom. They would take sheets, books, chairs, etc. and build elaborate tents and get their sleeping bags and sleep in them. They would pretend they were spies and this was their hideout, or that they were princesses and this was their castle. We heard giggles late into the night. We loved seeing how creative they could be in their tent design and how big they could make it. We had fun sneaking up on them and listening to the stories they created. Kids have amazing imaginations and I wish we had been better at helping them find ways to use them.

We also went camping from time to time, but, not too often because it was so hot in Florida and the bugs were always so bad for camping. But we did enjoy the few camping trips we went on and the memories we created. I know this is a favorite vacation activity for many families, who find state parks or other camping sites and go on weekends as well. My son takes several camping trips a year with his family.

I truly owe a debt of gratitude to the family who allowed us to use their beach home each summer for two weeks. They eventually sold that home, which was one of the worst days of my life. Just kidding, but it did change where we spent our vacation from then on. We no longer have a place like that to go every summer, but God has been good to help us locate affordable homes where we could take our kids and grandkids each summer. It's not always the same location, but we always enjoy ourselves, wherever we go.

Our kids also attended church camp every summer, which they always enjoyed. We believed in sending our kids to church camp, where they could get to know other kids and enjoy a spiritual focus in a great setting. They had wonderful experiences with summer camps from the time they were pre-teens throughout their teenage years.

I loved to take the kids for rides through the mountains when we lived in Conway, Arkansas. One time when Libby was busy, I took the kids for a ride in the woods along the edge of the Ozark Mountains. We took a dirt road off the highway that led to a creek bed that I followed to an old cemetery that dated back to the Civil War. The kids shot BB guns and my .22 rifle. We had so much fun. I've found it doesn't take much to entertain kids if we'll just spend time with them. They love parks, swimming, and walking through the woods, things that don't cost anything but a little time.

Life passes so quickly and you only have so many years to parent your children. Slow down and enjoy them. Turn off your phone, turn off the TV, and get outside into the fresh air. So much of what's on television is not good for our children; the values are not the values we want them to embrace. I'm concerned for families that only have family time around the TV. It's a poor substitute for enjoying outdoor activities with your kids. When you get outside you tend to get more exercise, which also contributes to healthier family relationships.

Our kids loved looking at their baby pictures, and loved for us to tell them about the funny things they did as kids. I bet that's true for your children as well. Watch their eyes as you tell them about things they did when they were younger and you'll see how special it is for them to hear the stories and know how much you enjoyed them.

One of our traditions was taking turns sharing what we were thankful for at the dinner table, especially at Thanksgiving. We would ask one of our children to start and then we'd go around the table and each one would take a turn. It was really special when my parents or Libby's were with us. It meant a lot to our kids to hear their grandparents tell what they were thankful for, and made them appreciative of all that they had. And we were thankful for the godly heritage they gave us and our children. This is a tradition we still carry on at Thanksgiving, a time when most of our family is together. It takes longer with so many of us around the table, but it really is special hearing our grandchildren express what they are thankful for.

We made a commitment when our kids were young for them to spend time with their grandparents. We had moved to Ft. Myers, Florida, which was eighteen hours from my parents' home in Arkansas, and another three hours to where Libby's parents lived in Waco, Texas. So we spent a week of our vacation divided between the two sets of parents. We always tried to get home at Christmas as well, but we were the youth pastors of almost four-hundred kids and we were always involved in the Christmas Eve service. But as soon as the service was over, generally about 8:30 p.m., we would get in the car and drive through the night to one of our parents' homes. We usually didn't arrive until noon the next day, but at least we were home. Again, we would split the week between both parents, then turn around and drive home.

Those were long, hard trips, but it gave our children the opportunity to spend time with their grandparents and other family members. It was worth the sacrifice to ensure that relationships were created and maintained between our kids and their aunts, uncles, cousins and grandparents. Our kids loved their grandparents, and as they grew older it was a blessing to see them interact with them. My children loved playing cards and being teased by my father. He was playful and he picked at the kids and endeared them to him. My mom spoiled them with goodies she had baked. Libby's parents were not card players, but they found a way to reach into the kids' hearts and bless them. The children developed deep and lasting relationships with our families.

Saturday morning at our house was pancake time. Every Saturday morning I made pancakes for the kids, and they loved it. I made Mickey

Mouse, Goofy and snowman pancakes. I used blueberries or chocolate chips for the eyes and mouth. The kids would get so excited to choose their characters and see how they turned out. It was our Saturday morning tradition. Their sleepover friends also enjoyed this time with us. I now do the same thing with our grandkids when we're together. I love to see the excitement in their eyes, and to hear their giggles as they wait for their pancakes to get done. It's another way of finding fun in family life.

I so appreciate the activities Libby did with our kids throughout the years, and how she continues to do that with our grandchildren. She always makes sure there are crafts and other things to entertain the kids before holiday dinners, and when they come to visit us as well. Libby makes a great MeMe. I know our grandkids would say the same.

Recently, she took our oldest granddaughter away for a few days, just the two of them, to teach her how to sew. I couldn't believe that she and Aniston made a scarf, a poncho and a hat in that short amount of time. Aniston so enjoyed her time with her grandmother, just the two of them, spending time and bonding together. Libby plans to do the same with each of our grandchildren on their tenth birthdays. What another great tradition for our family.

A Crazy Day at the Beach

As I'm sure you know by now, our family loves going to the beach, and there was one beach trip that was especially unforgettable. My sister had come for a visit and joined us on our beach excursion. Little did we know that our young daughters had gotten into their aunt's purse and eaten some of her chocolate Ex-Lax. It wasn't long after arriving at the beach that one of our girls came running up, saying, "I gotta go, I gotta go, I gotta go!" She had a desperation we had never seen before. I quickly picked her up and ran toward one of those portable outdoor bathrooms. As I pulled down the bottoms of her swim suit, she exploded. I didn't know it was possible for such a blast to come from my little girl. It went everywhere. To make matters worse, there was only a little toilet paper left on the only roll in the Porta-Potty. After my initial shock, I began to laugh. What else could I do? As a good dad, I wiped her little bottom with what toilet paper there was, but there wasn't much I could do to clean up the Porta-Potty. I pitied the next visitor to the toilet.

When I returned and told Libby and my sister what happened we did some investigating and discovered the problem. We laughed until we cried and then watched to see who might be the unfortunate beach goer to visit the toilet next.

Stories like this happen in every family, and if you have a funny bone in your body you just have to laugh at these crazy events. They may seem random, and they are, but that's the point. So laugh, especially at the things that could really upset you. I mean, I could have gotten angry at the antelope that drooled on me, on the orangutan that spit at me, and the snake that tried to bite me, but it would have ruined what turned out to be fun memories for our family. So learn to see the *fun* in *crazy*, and turn negative situations into memorable ones. That's how to find the fun in family life.

Surviving Childhood—What a Miracle!

I remember one childhood memory that sends chills through me now, and only by the grace of God did I survive. I was six years old and was playing hide-and-seek in the dark with my siblings and some neighborhood friends. We were having fun chasing each other around the house. Then it happened. My older brother decided to climb onto the top of the house and jump down onto a brick flowerbed that was home base. The flowerbed was about three feet high and four feet long. I was at base when my brother bailed off the house and landed on me, driving my head into the brick planter, creating a two inch gash at my hairline. I ran into the house with my face covered in blood.

My parents gasped then grabbed a towel to put pressure on the cut. We went immediately to the emergency room. I'll never forget the trauma of being six and having the doctor put a sheet over my entire body to view the cut through a small hole in the top of the sheet. It scared me to death. I've never forgotten that experience. Obviously I survived, but when I got older, the scarring of that injury turned into a cancerous mass that had to be cut out. I was the recipient of more pain as a result of my older brother's foolish move.

When I was nine years old we were once again playing hide-and-seek in the dark at my parents' fish camp on the lake. I made the mistake of climbing into the back of a flatbed truck when the boy who was "it" was about to get me. I jumped off the side of the truck with my mouth open only to get caught by the clothesline and found myself hanging by my teeth. My gums were ripped open and my teeth were sticking out in front of my mouth. I became instantly what the kids referred to as buck-toothed. My dentist quickly pushed and pulled them back in place with braces, which I had until I was a sophomore in high school. I laugh about it today and tell people that that accident made it possible for me to eat corn on the cob through a barbed wire fence. Once again I survived and I have pretty teeth today … with the help of twenty caps and a bridge.

Joe

<u>Having Children</u>

Eleven months into our marriage I came home from work on a Thursday for lunch. My dear wife looked at me with a bizarre expression. She had a piece of plastic in her hand. "It turned," was all she could mutter. "It turned? What turned?" She pointed to a box on the counter. The box read "Pregnancy Test." Well, I think we passed—or maybe we flunked, depending on your perspective—that particular test. I said, "Turn it back." But there was no turning back so we were thrust like a rocket into big boy and big girl responsibilities. Married for one month shy of a year, after dating four years, we got the shock of "family planning" without much of a plan. But I wouldn't change it for anything. The children have been fantastic.

Change happened dramatically even before the delivery of Joseph. Cecilia's parents, her dad a retired postman and her mom a retired accountant, sacrificially bought us a trip to Hawaii for our first anniversary. Out of seven days in paradise, four of them were spent in a hotel room for very unromantic reasons. Cecilia was retching from morning sickness. I knew life was going to be very, very different; and so it has been, wonderfully so.

But throughout that first pregnancy, I wondered if I could do it. Could I handle this entire child-raising thing? I had such a dysfunctional beginning in my own life that the thought terrified me. But as I was in prayer one day I had a thought I believe came from the Holy Spirit. It went like this: "The first minute of fatherhood you will have exercised more commitment than your own biological father. You most certainly can do it." A wave of assurance and even confidence swept over me. I knew then, and it has proven true, that *commitment* would be a very powerful resource.

Another feeling swept over me at the birth of my first child. Responsibility! Before March 4, 1988, the only person I had to feed was me.

Cecilia was an intelligent adult capable of ingenuity and survival. She could take care of herself if I fell off a cliff. This little human, on the other hand, needed constant help to exist. I was responsible to keep that little guy alive. Of course that responsibility was shared by my wife, and she was definitely hard-wired for motherhood.

It is my contention that the majority of credit—anywhere from 51% to 99%—for our well-adjusted children belongs squarely to Cecilia Griggs Phillips—and, of course, to our Sovereign Lord. Cecilia is amazing. She's been awesome since the children were in utero, when she began singing and praying over them without stop.

I'm happy to share for the first time in writing, and possibly for the first time publicly, my prayer for each of the children during our pregnancies. While they were "in the oven," I prayed these prayers almost daily. 1) I asked the Lord to allow the children to be perfectly formed in their mother's womb. I would often quote the Scripture from Psalm 139:13-15: *"For you created my inmost being; you knit me together in my mother's womb. I praise you because I am fearfully and wonderfully made; when I was made in the secret place..."* 2) I asked God to give the children perfect health. 3) I asked that the children be calm in spirit (that was a selfish request for my sleep!). And 4) I asked that each child would bring glory to God.

If you have no children yet, please be prepared to order some fruit. Read the fruit of the Spirit list in Galatians. Order all of them. Especially order patience. Sleep comes at a premium when babies come. Husbands, don't pretend to be asleep when the baby starts crying. At least don't pretend *every* time! Serve your wife by getting up with the baby. Give her some rest. Change the diapers. After all, you helped make that child. She did the heavy lifting by carrying, nurturing and delivering.

One fun memory I have is bringing home Madeline, the youngest of our four children. My friend David owns a limousine service. I asked him if I could hire him to bring Cecilia and me home with the baby. He gave us that service as a baby gift, so we brought her home in a long, white limousine. It was the first time I'd ever been in one. My secretary, Cindy, had a delicious Italian dinner prepared for the whole family when we arrived. I volunteered to take first shift for that first night home with Madeline. I knew the drill so I decided to make it enjoyable. I rented the movie *Shawshank Redemption*. I can never see that film advertised on television now without remembering that wonderful first night with our Maddie.

Fatherhood and motherhood are true commitments. Once, as a youth pastor in Georgia, I received a very memorable call. A businessman's secretary called the church and asked what I would charge to tutor her boss's son. I asked a few questions. Youth ministers are not exactly tutors, and I didn't feel qualified. The more I pressed the issue it became apparent the boss wasn't asking for tutelage. He didn't want a Big Brother or mentor for his son, nor was he looking for a spiritual guide. The boy was in trouble and the businessman was far too busy to get involved, so what he really wanted was to hire a *father*. After all, when you have money you can afford to buy goods and services of all types. But fatherhood? Sorry, but that's not something to be purchased. As much as I needed the money, there was no way I could have lived with myself if I had said anything to the secretary other than I what I did: "Ma'am, I can't be bought to father this young man. I can counsel. I can mentor. We can network relationships with some more mature students. We even have a parent support group. But the job you're looking for is *daddy*, and that's already been filled ... by your boss. Thank you and God bless."

Communication

Children. These little humans are sponges. They soak up everything from the environment in which they're raised. We've all seen little children on the internet imitate music conductors, singers, even preachers. They make us laugh when they act so grown up. The frightening thing is that, in reality, most of us act like our parents. I say in one of my comedy bits that I promised myself I wouldn't do the things my father did when I got really old, like in my thirties or super old, like in my forties. I wouldn't take a nap in the middle of the day for no good reason. I'd have to have diarrhea or a migraine or something. Now I *dream* about the opportunity for that forty-minute nap that eludes me in my current schedule. I promised not to hold my wife's purse in the mall. I flamed out on that promise as well. I promised not to watch news. Every night, my dad watched thirty minutes of local news followed by thirty minutes of national news, no matter what. What kind of life was that?! Now if I go an hour without news of some kind I start "Jonesing" for a news fix. You have the idea.

I imagine many readers do things they said they'd never do, perhaps even subconsciously, that they watched their parents do, that aggravated them to no end. The way we raise our kids forms the scaffolding for nearly all future behavior. I saw on the news last year a six-year-old child with a Kalashnikov rifle. He could barely hold it. Terrorists were discipling him to demonically hate certain people. Only the grace of a sovereign God could prevent that little boy from destroying people or even destroying himself when he grows up. What we communicate and how we communicate it has generational implications.

Billy Sunday has always intrigued and inspired me. He was an orphan who became a professional athlete, and then one of the best known evangelists in America in the early twentieth century. Athletics and fatherlessness have always been close to my heart, hence the attraction to Billy Sunday. As a child he spent a good amount of time at the Iowa Soldiers'

Orphans' Home in Davenport. His ministry was unorthodox and physical. I have a physical approach to my comedy and also cover a lot of the stage when I preach. I like that Billy was extremely successful. His obituary described him as "the greatest high-pressure, mass conversion Christian evangelist that America or the world has ever known." During his thirty-nine year career as an evangelist he undertook over 300 crusades. He preached nearly 20,000 sermons to over 100 million people (though Sunday did not preach to a hundred million different individuals, but to many of the same people repeatedly over the course of a campaign). Billy Sunday won tens of thousands of people to Jesus Christ. Literally, tens of thousands.

However, history reveals three important people who were not won to Christ—his three sons. Billy Sunday's sons were lavishly provided for. However, they were raised by strangers. The boys embarrassed their parents with outrageous lifestyles. All three died before the age of forty in tragic, violent deaths. George was arrested for public drunkenness and stealing automobiles. He committed suicide in 1932. Billy, Jr. died in an automobile accident in 1938. Paul, a test pilot, died in an airplane crash in 1944. Helen, their oldest child and only daughter, was happily married but developed a degenerative disease. She died of pneumonia in 1932. The boys put their parents through horrible grief and despair. Imagine these parents fighting for prohibition while their boys were lying in the streets drunk. This couple, so deeply involved in ministry, continued to deal with the drama of being extorted and blackmailed by the ex-wives of the boys. They were extorted publicly and they were extorted quietly. The exes wanted to be bought off for silence about the outrageous actions of the sons.

Successful football coaches film games and sometimes practices. Game film is a valuable resource and tool. The coach stands before the assembled squad. "Stop the tape! Rewind it. Now play it in slow motion. Johnson! See where you missed that block? How many times do you have to see this? You are supposed to pull on that play." Great biblical figures and historical characters serve as game film for me. "David! You shouldn't have been on the roof at the time when kings go out to war! You missed that block right there and it cost the game for a lot of people!" Billy Sunday and his wife "missed the block" when they employed people to do their job of raising their boys. I read once (cannot confirm but seems entirely plausible) that Billy Sunday won 90,000 people to Jesus in New York during one crusade. Ninety thousand is far more than three. Were any of those 90,000 more important to Rev. and Mrs. Sunday than their three sons? I submit NO.

Hear me, reader. I have purposed that I will not win the world to Jesus Christ at the expense of the humans that bear my name. Let me say it this way. I won't win everybody else's kids without making sure my kids go to heaven or at least do everything within my power to ensure that happens. I have joked to the kids as I raised them that they have a free will to choose or not choose Jesus. "If you choose not to follow Jesus, I will take you into the woods for three days with a roll of duct tape, a bottle of honey and a few fire ants. Duct taped to a tree, your worldview and theology might change!" (Relax Social Services, they knew I was joking!) The kids would laugh at my comments, but the truth behind the bluster was clear. If my kids got in the mud or weeds they knew I was deadly serious about the value of Christ in every person in our family. One of the ten things I regularly end my prayer time with is this: "My children all love God and they are going to serve Him all the days of their long lives." I am so serious about this that they grew up knowing I'd drop everything on my schedule and find them if they strayed. When I found them I would isolate them, love them, pray over them, fast for them, and utilize every tool to squeeze the "hell" out of them. Heaven only. Hell can't have you. That was and is my personal policy.

If you have kids or grandkids in the mud of sin let me offer some hope. Hear me, please. First, there is a great promise for you: *"Therefore, there is now no condemnation for those who are in Christ Jesus"* (Romans 8:1, NIV). Scripture calls Satan the accuser of the brethren. God was and is a perfect father, yet He has millions of rebellious children. Perhaps you have recently graduated from treatment and deeply regret that you didn't know Dr. Nance's principles of raising kids and you're concerned about your own children. I have good news. You can do the next right thing. God has the ability to press "control, alt, delete" and reset the screen with fresh opportunities and miracles. If your child is a wild and rebellious hellion, I bet you've struggled with the tension between the will of God and the free will of man. You know that God is not willing that any should perish. You also know man has a twisted nature that often chooses the broad path that leads to destruction. So why pray over the tension? How do I pray for this fight? I heard Dr. James Dobson say this once and I'm sure it has encouraged countless thousands with its truth: "Your child may have a free will, but God has a thousand ways to make them willing." Read it again. Think about it. Doesn't it ring true? Cling to this promise: *"And they said, Believe on the Lord Jesus Christ, and thou shalt be saved, and thy house"* (Acts 16:31, KJV).

Chores and Responsibilities

Dr. Nance admits he wasn't a perfect parent. But here, I have to hang my own head in shame. I should have done better when it came to chores and responsibilities. Cecilia and I never paid allowances to our kids. Perhaps that could have been thought through a little better. We did have some expectations that our kids would be responsible members of the family. "Take your plate to the sink" was one responsibility. "Make your bed" (hit or miss). "Rake out all the dead squirrels from your room or whatever is causing that smell." (Joke) Some of the kids were better at it than others. Ministry kept us at Mach 5 most of the time. Honestly, enforcing chores and responsibilities sometimes seemed like more work than doing them ourselves, and that is a patently wrong philosophy.

I liked the concept of pain and reward. I tended to "scorch the earth" in the pain phase, however. For example, I told my elementary-aged son several days in a row to make his bed. He's smart, has been his whole life, but he couldn't grasp the value or intellectual logic in making a bed that would be wrecked again a few hours later. I told him, "If you don't make your bed in the morning I won't register you to play soccer the entire season. Do you understand? Repeat it back to me." The next day the bed remained in wreck mode. He did not play soccer. Rather than a valuable teaching tool it got a little tedious answering all the questions that season, "Hey, why isn't your son playing soccer?" The answer, "He didn't make his bed one Tuesday morning," was light on bravado and heavy on curious.

Full disclaimer: Cecilia was much better at enforcing responsibility and accountability. "We have to keep them accountable, Joe." I didn't hear that a hundred times; no, I lost track after two hundred. But she was right. Accountability and responsibility were and are important. If a child is coddled, pampered or excused, they grow up believing the world works differently than it really does. Children are in for a rude awakening if they are reared in an entitlement paradigm. We didn't coddle or pamper our children. We—or should I say I—didn't do a great job with the structure and leadership part. We can't live in morbid introspection, but we can learn from mistakes and warn others when the bridge is out. Work ethic is crucial and all of my children have strong ones. Some only work hard at the things that interest them. The cold hard fact remains that some things are tedious and not interesting. But the boring things must be done in order to work hard at the things that are value-producing.

Effective Discipline for Pre-Teens

    I haven't observed the following scenario in quite a while. I used to hear it a lot more. Have you ever been in a store and a parent barked at his/her child, "Billy, put that candy bar back! I'm not kidding. Put it back." The kid just looks up with a defiant grin and continues to grip the chocolate. As the parent gets backed into the proverbial corner, you sense her tense up. She's been very public with her parental exhortation. Now there's a crowd; John Q. Public is looking on. How will she respond? What is the repercussion in this particular parent's administration for blatant disobedience? Am I the only parent who's heard another parent bellow, "One, two... Billy! One...two... I'm not kidding! One...! Two...! You don't want me to get to three, Billy! I mean it! One..." Then I scream from aisle eight, "Three! Three! There it is Billy, three!" At least I scream it in my mind. I'm not yet that bold or tactless. I'll wait until I get to be an old man because old people can say anything. There are a few obstacles with pre-teen discipline, and one of them is that too few parents get to "three." (Ironically, on the same day I wrote this I went to get an oil change. In the waiting room the exact scene I just described went down!)

    A marketing book I read a few years ago said that one way to train people is to show them a video of what *not* to do. I don't consider myself an expert at disciplining children. We did it. God helped us. They turned out great. I take no credit. I sincerely give the credit to God and I am grateful for Cecilia. I joked with someone just today about some friends I had who disciplined kids with very tight boundaries. Their child was never a minute late for his 8:30 p.m. bed time. His toys were always picked up. These parents were experts it seemed. Compared to them I felt like my rules were, "All right! Last cigarette out by midnight! You've got fifth grade advanced placement tests in the morning and we aren't going to be late again!" I hope my hyperbole is obvious to the reader. But all kidding aside, some of the experts' kids have broken their parents' hearts. Though not perfect, our kids have gladdened our hearts to date. I can't overemphasize the gratitude I have to the Lord for this.

I majored in psychology in college and I've been introduced at a military academy overseas as *the* American expert in psychology, but what I don't know about the subject would fill vast libraries. Even so, I offer a few do's and don'ts about discipline for your consideration:

Do NOT embarrass your children. When Jesus was dealing with a demon-possessed kid in Mark 9, he saw that a crowd was running to see the show, and in my mind Jesus delivers the child before the gaping sightseers got there. Jesus is not into embarrassing children and we shouldn't be either. DO discipline your child privately. If he does something squirrelly in public, do everything within your power to remove him from the stage and take care of the behavior away from gaping sightseers.

Do NOT punish. I don't consider discipline to be punishment. Punishment by definition is "to subject to pain, loss, confinement, death, etc., as a penalty for some offense, transgression, or fault." I considered our discipline to be *correction*. Correction by definition is "the action or process of correcting something; a change that rectifies an error or inaccuracy." If a child exhibits disobedient or anti-social behavior, then the result is an action which will impact future behavior positively. DO correct. The prisons are filled with men and women incarcerated for crimes. Redemption is in short supply in most institutions. Our discipline is intended to redeem.

Do NOT be stupid. I've heard of parents grounding their kids from church and even making them read the Bible or write verses over and over. That's mind boggling! And it sure seems counterproductive to me. The Bible is always to be honored and highly valued. To equate punishment, discipline or even correction to that honored book seems unwise. Bible memory exercises should be joyful. I would never want my child to associate the inspired Word of God with tedium or drudgery. Utilize the truths of the Bible within the correction if you desire. "See how this was wrong, Billy? We read this Proverb. Did you do this or did you do something else?" That sort of thing. DO use wisdom. If your church has a good youth ministry, don't ground your kids from participating, ground them from the movies or some such thing. If your values are undergirded by the youth service, pick another thing to picket.

Do NOT hurt children. I'm not talking about corporal, tempered and appropriate correction on the hindquarters. I'm talking about hitting, shaking, throwing, or pushing children. It may have happened to us and we say, "Didn't bother me. I turned out okay." This seems basic but the golden rule applies: Whatever you want people to do to you, do to them. I think the rule works in reverse as well. Did you want to be pushed down and punched? We should not do that to our children either. DO correct in a way that is not harmful.

Do NOT play games when it comes to discipline. Children should never wonder about the love the parent has for them. Perhaps the correction goes like this. "Lisa, you were told not to put the cat in the fish tank, weren't you? Tabby is wet because you disobeyed, isn't that right? You know that your disobedience has to be corrected, right? I don't want to pop your bottom, but because I love you I have to correct you. This will be over in a minute, but you will feel it. I want you to know Mommy loves you very much and that is why I am correcting you for nearly drowning our pet, not to mention that it ate another pet while in the tank." Give the swat. Let her process it and cry. When appropriate time has elapsed (varies for different personality types—five minutes or fifty-five minutes), return to her room and hug it out. Offer an activity together. Make some brownies or play something. It's over. Don't hold it over the head of the child. Don't bring it back up over and over again, and for the love of heaven, don't bring it up in front of others. The butt of our jokes should not be our children. Some parents pout worse than their kids, and give them the cold shoulder. They play games. Some experts assert that one beauty of the "spare the rod, spoil the child" discipline philosophy is that there is a finality to it. "Whew, that's over; let's get on with the day." Emotional sabotage takes place when the adult can't let it go. DO let your yes be yes and your no be no and move on.

Fun Things We Did with Our Kids

Joseph was our gym rat. I was a basketball coach and that was a glorious time for our six-year-old boy. He was like the team mascot. He walked down the hill from the big Christian elementary school he attended and came to practice every day. The older boys were his heroes. They treated Coach's little boy as their little brother. Jeremy Denton was our starting sophomore point guard on that team. Now he is a professor at my alma mater and my youngest is the nanny for his five children in Florida. That has been a really cool and fun development in the family.

Families that are healthy seem to have inside jokes. Not the inside jokes that are cruel to others or make other people feel stupid. For example, there is a collective groan when we watch a movie together because somewhere during the movie, Dad (me) is going to make a statement. I will pick my spot. Preferably, the spot will be during the most outrageous scene: man jumps from helicopter to helicopter in the air, aliens morph into a poodle, that type of thing. I will say, "Y'all know this is based on a true story. It happened in Des Moines, Iowa, in 1969." Groan. I have no idea why I continue to torture my family with this nonsensical statement, but I do so in 93% of the movies we watch together.

Our family has a unique vernacular. It is not a unique language. We speak English or a replica of it. We say things like this: "Come on, Carl." "How ya doin', Tommy?" "Real nice." "Happy Birthday, Maddie." "That shot was real nice." "Da da da da da" and dozens of other statements that would mean nothing to other people. But they mean something to *us*. Often they are attached to a particular person or time period. We have threatened for years to make a family T-shirt of these ridiculous phrases. I think it would be fun and funny, but only to us. This project has not been launched as of yet.

One of the fun things we do happens at Christmas. I don't remember how this got started, but every Christmas we play hours of the card game Rummy. We try to play at other times as well, but mostly it's at Christmas. I suppose it has something to do with Grandma coming up from Florida. We love to play—though I admit I don't necessarily enjoy playing with slow players. We have, ahem, a couple of slow players in the family. But my love for being with some free-wheeling Phillips people trumps my disdain for card sloth. Rummy at the holidays is a lot of fun.

For much of our lives we were a pet-free zone. Sixty-seven percent of the Phillips family is allergic to pet hair. Like eyes-watering-and-swelling-half-shut allergic. But when Madeline was in second grade she found an abandoned beagle with a rope tied around a random chair in the Ohio village we lived in. We had just watched the movie *Because of Winn Dixie* when she found the dog. She named it Dixie and brought it home. Because the movie was fresh in our minds, we were open to the idea of having a dog. So we bought some pet paraphernalia … and plenty of allergy medication. About a week into this pet project Dixie got into a fight with the German shepherd in the neighbor's back yard. She lost the fight in a decisive fashion. I gathered her up and rushed her to a nearby veterinarian. The vet said it would cost $2,000 to surgically fix the dog. He was speaking to a man who had spent a cumulative twenty-five cents in fifteen years on pets. So my response was, "How much for the shot program?" "The shot program?" He was clearly confused. "Yes, the put-down shot." (I had not yet become attached to Dixie at that point.) "Twelve dollars," he said. I could tell I'd lost some esteem in his eyes. "Well, Doc, here's the deal. It isn't even officially my dog. I'll let you choose. I'll give you $12 or $200. For $200, I want the surgery and I want you to neuterize, vaporize, simonize or whatever you have to do so that dog doesn't become a parent. I want you to throw in the shots as well. Your choice." He negotiated my offer to $225, which I was willing to pay. We had years of enjoyment with Dixie. The dog reminded me of some church people: perfect in the house, but it ran wild as soon as it got out the door. We moved from Ohio to Charlotte, NC, and one day Dixie chased a rabbit and never came back.

We went through a cat phase too. It was horrible. Don't get me wrong. I like cats... they taste like chicken. Forgive me for that bad joke. I know, it was very poor taste. Where were we? Oh, yes, one day Cecilia was walking to the garage. I said, "Where are you going with that bowl of milk?" "To the garage." "No, drink your milk in here and put it in a glass ... wait a minute! I know what you're doing! Are you feeding an animal?" "Yes, but it's pitiful. It's a cat. I'm just going to give it a drink and it'll be on its way." Uh, huh. I suppose the reader knows the end of that story. It was most assuredly not on its way. It was now on its stay. But I got the last laugh. This Egyptian-looking cat was a magnificent huntress. It was killing things left and right and would often leave a portion of the kill at the front door. Rabbit head. Headless bird. Watching my wife call on the name of the Lord when she encountered these carcasses was sheer joy. The cat, Goldie, had three litters of kittens during that cat phase of the Phillips' history. On stage I follow that statement with this deadpan, "And we didn't raise the cat that way. We used to take her to little kitty VBS and put her little paws together in prayer." I took the cat to the same veterinarian to get it vaporized, neuterized, simonized or whatever. Each time, the doc said, "Can't do it. She's expecting." My oldest son would look at me as his eyes watered profusely from an allergic reaction and say something like, "Have you ever loved me? I hate these cats." I went everywhere looking for ways to get rid of the cats. I went to a cat shelter asking for help. "We don't take cats and there is really no one in the county that will. Call next week and I'll try to help you find somewhere in North Carolina, but it's really hard. I can't help you today because I am preparing for our annual fundraiser." I saw a crack in the door. "Who is your entertainment at the event you're hosting?" "We have no entertainment." "Here are some references, ma'am. My services have been acquired for thousands of dollars in the past (maybe a couple of times I was acquired at that rate so it wasn't a lie). I'm willing to donate a show to you if you'll take these cats off of my hands forever." I'm not necessarily proud of this, but I prostituted out my comedy ability (or lack thereof) to rid the family of a bunch of bouncing little allergens.

Our newest and perhaps greatest pet is a Shih Tzu poodle named Ellie. I gave it to the family on Christmas several years ago. She's been a wonderful companion for Cecilia while I travel. Best of all, Ellie is hypoallergenic. The family loves her and she has brought immense joy to our home. Fun, fun, fun.

The Crazy Day

Crazy is not a politically-correct word, but it is a biblical word, sort of. I have very close biological relatives who have been diagnosed with some serious mental illnesses. A few others should be diagnosed! I recently told a crowd in Alabama that if I had unlimited resources I'd keep a psychiatrist on retainer. Occasionally, I would call him/her and say, "Meet me at Waffle House for a twenty-five minute tune-up. Just a look-see over some smothered and covered hash browns." So I don't use words like "crazy" flippantly. Regardless of the politically-incorrect terminology, read these verses from 1 Samuel: "*Therefore he [David] changed his behavior before them and pretended to be insane in their hands. And he scratched on the doors of the gate and let his spittle run down his beard. Then said Achish to his servants, 'You see the man is acting like a madman. Why then have you brought him to me? Am I one who lacks lunatics, that you brought this one to behave as a madman in my presence? Will this man come into my house?'*" (1 Samuel

21:13-15, MEV). I'm considering making this verse my theme for next year: "Do I lack lunatics …?"

Lunacy was modeled to David by his boss, Saul, a boss, by the way, who tried over and over to kill him, a boss David went out of his way to honor and protect even after Saul was dead. It was apparent that holding the sword of Goliath on Main Street of Gath (Goliath's hometown) could be a death sentence. David had to make a split-second decision. Like James Bond or Jason Bourne, he had to act fast to save his life. His brothers had acted crazy. His sheep had acted crazy. Sheep would just walk over a cliff in mental oblivion. His boss demonstrated some strong lunacy. In a crazy world sometimes you just have to lean into the lunacy a little bit. We have to let the insanity inform us. David scratched at the doors of the gate and drooled into his beard. If the world's gone crazy, get something out of it! King Achish was astonished. Perhaps he felt like Jack Nicholson in the 1997 film *As Good As It Gets,* who famously said, "Sell crazy somewhere else; we're all stocked up here." So the king let David live. Don't waste all of the crazy in the crazy days.

Jerry wrote about a crazy day at the beach his family experienced. There have been plenty of those for the Phillips family, whether at the beach or at home. Raising four kids with a brave, strong wife who has suffered with type-1 diabetes and other health challenges ensured some different days. A holiday season in Macon, GA, a few years ago stands out because Cecilia was in the I.C.U. at the local hospital. The kids were young and juggling school and extra-curricular stuff. I was "going it alone" and decorating was not at the top of the survival list. But Cecilia was turning a corner and hope was on the rise. There was no way I wanted to bring her home just before Christmas to no Christmas cheer, so I went to a local Christmas tree lot to see if there were any trees left. Of course, the trees had been picked over, but there were a few pitiful ones left, so I got the best of the worst for the exorbitant price of … 75 cents. Since we could get Christmas trees for less than a dollar, I decided to get two! So that year Cecilia came home to two Christmas trees!

That holiday also brought an interesting Christmas Eve worship experience. I said to the kids, "Mom is doing well and resting. The neighborhood church is having a candlelight communion service. It will probably be short, so let's go and thank the Lord that Mom's home." The pastor spoke that evening on the genealogy of Jesus found in the Gospel of Luke. He read dozens of names and connected them to the virgin birth like a professor's lecture in a university classroom. It was akin to an infamous college course that one would have heard about and wanted to avoid! My five-year-old son was using my leg as a pillow within the first four minutes. As the lecture groaned on and on, Kennon exhaled the loudest, most exasperated yawn imaginable. I couldn't get my hand over his mouth fast enough. Time stood still as everyone in the sanctuary whipped their heads in my direction. Of course, they couldn't see the little boy with his head on my knee. The pastor looked up, puzzled momentarily, then went back to reciting name after name. But to my surprise, heads began to bob across the crowd. "I'm with that kid," was my interpretation of their body language. Following the eternal service, awkwardness ramped up to another level. It was time for communion in this protestant church, but they weren't going to receive it in a protestant way. No wafers and no tiny cups. Instead, there was a common cup at the front of the church. A hundred or more people stood in line for a shared cup of sugary grape juice and a pinch of bread. I graciously allowed people ahead of my big family. "Go ahead. Step back, kids. You go. No, after you. Go to the back, kids. Let these good folks pass." And as soon as we backed our way out of the sanctuary and into the lobby I told the kids to make a break for it! For some reason I didn't want to be the 101st person sipping sugary juice at the bottom of a common cup. Call me crazy. And yep, that was a crazy day.

Sometimes crazy days can only be described as evil and desperate days. "Mr. and Mrs. Phillips, I'm not sure Madeline will make it through this. There's a good chance she'll die. If she does live, she'll probably have brain damage." The doctor took Cecilia and me into a little conference room when he delivered that information about our recently-delivered daughter. Madeline was just three weeks old. Presbyterian Hospital was our third hospital. Maddie had an olive complexion, we thought. The reality was that she had Respiratory Syncytial Virus (RSV), which had caused that hue to her skin. RSV presents like a common cold but has devastating and frequently-terminal results in infants. The *crazy* day rocketed to an *evil and desperate* day. I can't tell you how devastated we were at the news. The hospital was about thirty miles from our house. Cecilia spent every night at the NICU in three different hospitals, while I'd go home in the evening to care for our three other young children. Work and life continued, but we were numb, just going through the motions.

One night we were in a "step-down" room, a level just under NICU, and a cleaning lady walked in, thinking the room was empty. She had a glow about her. She was actually singing before she saw us. When she turned around, she jumped at being startled by our presence. Cecilia was holding Madeline, and the woman apologized profusely for disturbing us. Cecilia said it was no problem. The lady asked, "Are you folks okay tonight?" She seemed genuinely concerned. Cecilia said, "We are. The Lord has been very good to us." Without the slightest hesitation she said, "Ain't that the truth?!" then went on to say, "I was just telling my girlfriends up here on the crew that God is so good to us. I'm so happy y'all know about the goodness of God." The room seemed to light up with the glory of the Lord. I thought revival might break out. I've never forgotten her reaction, and that was twenty years ago. I hope I never forget her reaction.

God did a great work in Madeline's life. Not only did she survive, there was no brain damage. Just the opposite. She graduated as an honored scholar. She was the state Jr. Bible Quiz Champion. She twice was winner of best preacher for the state of North Carolina. Madeline was the lead in the production of *Annie Get Your Gun,* singing fourteen songs. I drive by that hospital quite often. I remember that the Lord was very good to us.

The Bible says, *"Wherefore take unto you the whole armor of God, that ye may be able to withstand in the evil day, and having done all, to stand"* (Ephesians 6:13, KJV). When the crazy and evil days come don't give in to the temptation to be overwhelmed. Stand. Just like getting a shot of medicine, the pain will eventually pass. Family is so important. Lean into each other and stand against those storms.

CHAPTER 5

PARENTING TEENAGERS

Jerry

This topic deserves its own chapter. What an interesting time in the life of a family when the kids pass through the teen years. If you have a teen right now, be encouraged. I wrote the words "pass through" on purpose. The teen years do end. There is a time limit on all the crazy that happens during those years between eleven and eighteen. I truly enjoyed this time in our kids' lives as we watched their personalities develop. If you're a dad with one or more daughters, you'll have to learn to not react to their emotional ups and downs. I have found that if I just listen—and ask for help from my wife on what is the proper reaction or response—it works out better.

More than any time in your parenting role, this is the time to listen. Teens need parents who will listen to them and spend time with them when they are in the mood to spend time with you. Teens sometimes pull away for a season, trying to become their own person, and because of the influence of their friends at school. This is an awkward time for them and you, but you need to be there for them. I believe in time you'll find they won't abandon the relationship they had with you as pre-teens.

Moms and dads have a hard time when their kids act like they don't need them. I would suggest you keep an eye on this and that you and your mate devise a game plan to follow. If you begin to notice your child pulling away there are things you can do to help them feel comfortable finding themselves.

You might suggest they take a night or two away at a church event, or at a friend's house, or on an extended missions trip. Help them through this time and don't overreact when they try to spread their wings. Give them some grace while they find themselves. Be patient, loving, listen, and the teenage years will be over before you know it. Once they reach their twenties you'll be amazed how much your child acknowledges what you know and what they learned from you. I'm not kidding; your teens will seem to grow up overnight. The conversations you'll have will be so refreshing.

We had three wonderful children who each had their own unique personality that we so enjoyed. Yes, there were a few challenges, like every family experiences, but we passed through that time and our kids matured into wonderful young adults.

Chores in the Teen Years

As I said in Chapter 4, we expected our kids to keep their rooms clean. That wasn't optional. Libby and I both love a clean home, and we wanted to teach our children to appreciate and care for the things God has given us, and to respect things that belonged to other members of the family. But this created a challenge with each child. May I say you should thank God in heaven if you have a child who is a neat freak?

One of our children was of the "relaxed-room" philosophy, which drove her mother nuts. She wasn't purposefully rebellious; she just didn't mind clutter or clothes on the floor. It created a constant argument between the two of them. I finally said to Libby one day, "Don't pick up anything in her room and don't wash any clothes that aren't in the clothes hamper." I said, "Honey, don't worry about the carpet. When she leaves for college we'll take it out and replace it and repaint the room. Just ask her to keep her door closed when we have guests over."

That took so much pressure off of my wife when she agreed to not make a big deal of it. It was a rewarding morning when I overheard my daughter say to her mom, "I don't have anything clean to wear." Libby asked, in a calm respectful tone, "Did you put your dirty clothes in the laundry basket? I washed everything in the clothes basket." There was no fuss, no fight, just the realization that if her dirty clothes weren't in the hamper, they wouldn't get washed. Problem solved.

Through their teen years we carried on the practice that each child took a night to help with the dinner dishes. We tried to have dinner together as often as possible so we could share about our day and talk about what was coming up for the weekend and beyond. We talked about schoolwork and other things, but the key word is we *talked*. Then each child took their turn helping with the dishes, which took some of the load off of Libby. I helped as well from time to time to give my wife a break.

They also continued to help with housework on Saturday mornings, such as dusting and vacuuming, and they helped me do yard work and wash our cars. We always held to the conviction that each of us was responsible to contribute to the good of the family. That meant that we all helped with the work around the house. This never became a big issue. Everyone got it. Because we had instilled these values early in their lives, they didn't question it later.

Rules and Discipline

Curfews

We had a 10 p.m. curfew for our teenagers during the week and an 11 p.m. curfew on weekends unless there was a special event that justified later nights out. We also had to know where they were going while they were out. We lived in Orlando, Florida, and we wanted to be sure our kids were safe.

We understand that we didn't always know where they were when they were riding around with friends, but we never let them go with people we didn't know.

Some of their friends were surprised that our kids had a curfew, but that encouraged the friends to hang out at our house if they wanted to be with our daughters and son. It did help that we had beautiful girls and a handsome son. The guys understood why I would have a curfew.

When discipline was necessary, we sometimes restricted the use of the phone, which they all hated. We also kept them from going to an event as another means of discipline. These always got their attention.

Tattoos

My son was the only one of my children who asked us to let him get a tattoo. I know this is a personal conviction and parents have to decide for themselves how they handle the subject. I was persuaded that the tattoo you were inclined to put on your body at eighteen might not be one you would want later in life. So when my son began talking about getting a tattoo, I would simply answer, "Sure you can get a tattoo, but if you're man enough to get a tattoo, you're man enough to live on your own." When he graduated high school and continued the subject, I would say, "Sure you can get a tattoo, but if you're man enough to get a tattoo, you're man enough to pay for your own college education." He heard this time and again throughout his college years.

I did what I thought would keep him from a bad decision at an early age. I think everyone should wait until they are bit older than 18 to get a tattoo, because by the time you're in your twenty's, you're mature enough to celebrate that you didn't put *I love Sally* on your arm ... now that you're dating Ruth. Fads come and go, and while my viewpoint may be considered conservative, even old-fashioned, I feel tattoos are best considered later in life. This would save many a young person the money and regrets of having something tattooed on their bodies they later wish they hadn't.

Now, I have many good friends who have tattoos, and I have no problem with that. I just didn't want my son to make a decision he'd later regret, and I did whatever I could to help prevent that until he was at an age to make a mature decision. He doesn't have a tattoo … that I know of. Now, for all of you with tattoos, whose feelings are hurt, please know I was only trying to protect my son from impulsive decisions that he might later regret. I know some of you have amazing tattoos, because I've seen them, and I'm happy you're happy with your tattoo. So forgive me and go get yourself another tattoo in my honor. Just kidding.

Connecting with Your Teen

It's so important that parents find ways to connect with their teenagers and keep lines of communication open with them. Find things in common to talk about and activities you can enjoy together. It can be exercise, sports, band, art or some other interest, but show up. Be there for the ball games, or whatever else they're involved in. Celebrate their wins and encourage them in their losses.

Teen mood swings are real and I can say from experience that it can be difficult to talk with them when their moods are out of kilter. At such times they can seem impossible to reason with.

Our teens can be influenced by their friends and may bring home contrary thoughts and ideas to test on you. Try not to overreact when they do. Discuss these ideas with them, take time to consider them, and give them time to do the same. Showing respect for them as they test their wings is often enough to help guide them to right decisions.

Many teens dream of walking across Europe, Africa or Asia before starting college or during semester breaks. This sounds romantic and adventurous, and it is. We know there are lots of issues to be discussed with such an idea, and lots of things that can go wrong. Again, don't overreact. Not every idea your teen proposes is one he or she will act on. Be careful your response doesn't push them into something that was just an idea they were testing.

Again let me say, learn to communicate with your teen, and learn to listen. Don't put them off when they want to talk. There is no such thing as an inopportune time when it comes to communicating with your child.

A principle I like to talk to parents about is the Law of the Harvest. If you have a rebellious child who is using drugs or alcohol, or is getting in trouble with the law, you may want to consider this principle. The Law of the Harvest says that you reap what you sow! If you as a parent do the reaping for your child instead of letting them reap according to their actions, you violate the Law of the Harvest. Your child needs to experience the consequences of their bad decisions and behaviors. It may mean you leave them in jail overnight, or you let them get kicked off their sports team or expelled from the school they want to attend. Your child needs to feel the pain. If you constantly rescue them (and play God), they'll never know what it means to reap what they sow. You only extend the problem that can grow into other lifelong addictions and dysfunctional behaviors.

Pain is a major part of the process of learning from bad decisions. You must let your child experience that consequence early in life. It's far better for your child to experience a degree of pain for their actions, than for them—and you—to experience a lifetime of suffering for their bad decisions.

I just saved you years of grief if you will only listen to this advice and stop enabling your child. You can now buy another one of these books for one of your friends to repay me for such good advice.

Funding the Fun for Your Teen

As our children were growing up, Libby and I agreed our kids would use the money they worked for to pay for ski trips, concerts, movies and excursions with their youth group and friends. We would pay for summer camp and help fund their missions trips. Those trips tended to be expensive, but it was well worth the investment, as it gave them a chance to experience new cultures and expand their worldview. We felt these were critical trips to help our kids learn to give of themselves to people in other countries. This gave them a chance to minister with their peers and get acquainted with people and cultures around the world.

This method of funding activities worked out pretty well in that it helped the kids prioritize which events they really wanted to spend their money on. There were times we wanted the kids to attend something they couldn't afford so we would pitch in, but generally it was a good plan. Of course, we paid for dinners, movies and other activities when we went out as a family.

I mentioned in an earlier chapter that we were a family that enjoyed playing table games. We played card games like Uno, Rook, Shanghai Rummy, Spades, 3-13, a game called 7's and other card games. We made this a fun time with popcorn, desserts and drinks, and kept it light and fun. We had done this so often in the pre-teen years that when the kids grew older they continued to enjoy card games. They would bring their teenage friends over to play as well. Our home became the spot to hang out, which is just how we wanted it. It was much better than wondering where our kids were and what they were doing. We often went to bed and let the kids stay up late playing, laughing and didn't care if they were loud, because of the peace of mind we had in knowing our kids were enjoying themselves in a safe environment.

This may sound like over-parenting to some of you, but we gave them plenty of opportunity to go to their friends' homes, to go to school events, and attend youth events at the church. But they brought their friends to our house because they knew they would have a good time. We had a big screen TV that also attracted the youth to the house to watch movies. I can often remember coming out of my room to a den full of teens watching a movie and enjoying themselves. And usually this led to a sleepover, and I became the pancake man the next morning, feeding a herd of teens.

The Dating Game

Wrong boyfriend or girlfriend: WOW! I can tell you as the father of two beautiful daughters and a handsome son that this was a matter of prayer for Libby and me from the time they were two or three years old. We prayed often for their future mates and believed God would bring the right person into their lives. We wanted mates that would cherish them as we did, and who had values that would bring the blessings of God on their families.

I remember when 12-year-old boys began to show up at my front door wanting Denee' and Kristi to come out and play. I was shocked that these boys were on my front porch, asking if my girls could come outside with them. My first reaction was to sic our dog on them. The girls were growing up and I knew then that we were headed into some interesting years.

Libby and I decided that our kids could not date until they were sixteen, and the rule was we had to meet their dates before they went out with them. Furthermore, their dates had to spend an evening with our family so we could get to know them. That may sound extreme, but in our minds, we were protecting our kids from someone who might potentially hurt them.

As each of my daughters turned sixteen, I took her on her first date.

Weeks ahead, I told her she could pick the restaurant we would go to and that she could order whatever she wanted. I made the reservations and got set for the evening. Libby and I bought each girl a purity ring that I would give them on our date. When the special day came, I dressed up, bought flowers for my daughter, then drove back to the house and knocked on the front door.

As my "date" and I walked to the car I opened the door for her and we drove to the restaurant. As we were eating I asked a couple of questions I had prepared. I started with, "What characteristics do you want in the person you date and eventually marry?" Then I would listen as my daughter began to describe the traits she wanted in a boyfriend and husband. My oldest daughter mentioned several attributes like, "Someone who has goals, who is personable, who doesn't have a temper. In fact, someone just like you, Daddy." The words touched me deeply, then after a brief pause she added, "But someone with patience." Ouch.

I gave them each their ring and asked them to commit to staying pure and saving themselves for their husbands. I know by the world's standards this seems strange, but we wanted them to make good decisions when it came to how they selected their future mates. I also happen to believe that your honeymoon is one of the most special times in your life. If you've kept yourself pure, the experience is even more wonderful as you share with your mate the gift of love. To a similar degree, when someone who isn't a virgin becomes a new Christian and begins to date, they can commit to purity in a new relationship and know a measure of the reward of waiting. I know this isn't the norm in today's society, but those who are disciplined in their sex life prior to marriage will enjoy the fruit of their discipline.

Likewise, Libby took Dustin on his first date, and they too had a great conversation about what he was looking for in a girlfriend and future mate.

When boys began to come to our house to date our girls, I would suggest they bring ice cream when they came. This seemed like a fair trade to me if a guy wanted to spend time with my daughter. At first they would laugh, but the smart ones began to show up at the house with ice cream, and one even called ahead to ask what kind he should buy. We laugh about it today, because that young man is my son-in-law and the father of four of my granddaughters. From time to time, he still brings ice cream when he comes over. He gets it. Ice cream is my love language. I believe God must really love my daughter and son-in-law to honor them with four girls. They're great parents, and Libby and I are very proud of them.

I remember the first time a young man came to pick my daughter up for a date. I took him on a tour of my gun collection. I asked him where they were going, told him what time he would have my daughter home, and how I expected him to behave. This young man said, "Yes sir," over and over. I'm six feet, two inches tall, and towered over most of the boys who dated our daughters. I always enjoyed watching them the first time I met them. They would look up to me and I could see the caution come over them as I spoke to them. I had seen most of them at church and knew their families. And they had been in our home with other kids prior to dating my daughters.

I never went to sleep until my kids were home from their dates. With the date rape crimes I read about so often, I'm glad I had a conservative and cautious view of dating for my kids. We didn't have anything crazy happen during the dating years, and I thank the Lord.

One special memory I have was when Denee' was in college and a young man came to the house to spend the evening with her. As we talked I asked him what he was majoring in and he said, "English." I said, "That's great, what do you plan to do with your English degree? Are you thinking pre-law?" He said, "Well, sir, I just want to be liquid." I sat there thinking to myself, *what in the world does that mean, to be liquid*? To me that meant he didn't want to be committed to anything, so I said to him, "Son, I need you to help me understand what you mean by *being liquid*." He said, "Well, I want to spend some time traveling across Europe, teach for a while, weigh my options, take a job here for a while and there for a while and then decide." As far as I was concerned he was nailing his own coffin shut when it came to dating or marrying my daughter. I was hoping Denee' would drop him like a rock, and in fact, I challenged her about his answer after he left. He was a fine young man and very talented, but his concept of a work ethic ran against the grain of this father. He did not become my son-in-law. But I didn't sabotage his chances, he did.

Cars and Drivers' Licenses

Oh boy, what an interesting time it is when your teen gets his or her driver's license. (Check out my gray hair if you don't believe me.) We helped our kids get their first used car when they were old enough to drive. It was such a relief to make the deal with our oldest daughter. When we decided on a vehicle, we said, "If we get this car for you, you have to take your brother and sister to school and help drive them to sports practices and other activities." She quickly said yes, and what a help that was for Libby not to have to drive them everywhere.

Naturally, we laid out some rules when it came to their cars. One rule was that if they wrecked their car they had to pay the insurance deductible to have it fixed, which with our policy, was $500. That rule served its purpose because the first time one of my kids had an accident and saw their precious money go out the window to get their car fixed, it taught them to be more careful behind the wheel, which is what mattered most to us, of course. But having to pay for their mistake was an excellent teaching tool.

They also had to pay for their own gas unless we asked them to drive their siblings somewhere. That reminds me of when I was a teenager. More than once my twin brother and I siphoned gas from our sister's car and put it in my tank. Amazingly, she never caught on. The new gas tanks make that harder to do these days, which is a good thing.

Surviving the Teen Years

I survived a lot of crazy things when I was growing up. One of the craziest happened when I was twelve or thirteen years of age. My twin brother and I, along with our parents, were visiting some of their friends who happened to own a farm. Terry and I were looking for something to do outside and saw this Brahma bull standing in the pasture, eating grass. We had seen bullfighters on TV and wondered what that would be like. So we crawled under the barbed wire fence and walked out into the field.

The bull paid no attention to us until we started throwing rocks at his rear end, then it didn't take long to get a reaction. The bull turned toward us, ducked his head, and began to stomp one hoof and then the other. The dust began to fly, then he lowered his shoulders and got ready to charge.

That's when the lights came on in the minds of two young boys who were about to get trampled. We took off running about the time the bull lunged forward and charged after us. The barn was closer than the fence so we ran into the barn and scurried up a ladder that led to a loft. As we got to the top of the ladder, which was built into the wall, the bull began to ram it. The walls shook, in fact the entire barn shook. We ran to a corner of the loft to hide from the bull. He kept ramming the wall for what seemed like an eternity. We weren't sure the loft was going to stand. Finally, the bull lost interest and moseyed back out to the pasture.

We were so scared we didn't look down for a good thirty minutes or more. Then we worked up the nerve to try to see where he was. We looked through knot holes in the wood, and through cracks between planks, and finally saw that the bull had gone back to grazing. That was a relief, but we stayed where we were for another thirty minutes. Then I managed to talk Terry into climbing down the ladder to see if we could make a run for the fence. He said he thought we could, so I climbed down and followed Terry to the double-door entrance of the barn. The bull was looking the other way so we made a run for it. But the bull saw us and took out after us again. Terry and I hit the ground and scampered under the fence and ran as fast as we could to the house. The bull ran up to the fence, and thankfully, he stopped, because I'm not sure the fence would have held if he'd wanted to run through it.

We burst through the doors of the house, startling the adults. My folks asked what was wrong, and Terry and I both said, "Nothing, we were just racing to see who was the fastest." If we'd told our parents what we'd done, we'd have been in big trouble. But trust me, we had learned our lesson and didn't need a lecture or discipline.

Believe me when I say I haven't thrown a rock at a bull's rear end from that day to this and I don't recommend it to anyone. God was merciful and our guardian angels worked overtime and needed rest after that caper.

We learn some lessons the easy way and some the hard way. I learned one lesson I never forgot at the expense of my twin brother. We were six years old, and Terry and I were sitting on the porch with our Cocker Spaniel, Lucky. All of a sudden Terry lifted Lucky's ear and blew into it really hard. In the blink of an eye, Lucky turned and bit Terry right through the lip. It happened so fast Terry couldn't stop it. Instantly, blood began to pour down his chin and he let out a scream of pain I'll never forget. I learned that day not to blow into a dog's ear. Terry wasn't so *lucky*; he learned that lesson the hard way.

You may be thinking, "I'm glad I survived my teen years, in spite of the foolish things I did, but how do I navigate my own kids through their teen years?" Listen, all kids are different and you may not have many challenges at all from your teenagers. That's not the norm, but we can all hope.

Let me suggest you start with prayer. Pray hard and pray often. Pray that God protects your kids from making foolish decisions that might hurt them. Pray that God keeps them from using drugs and/or alcohol and protects them from people who promote a lifetime of bad habits. Pray for the favor of God on their lives and then leave them at the altar. You have to trust God to help them and help you. This is one of the most important times in life to learn to trust God.

Let me also suggest that you keep a close eye on their behavior. Who are they hanging out with and how they are spending their time? If you spend a normal amount of time with your child, you'll know when something isn't right. Do they shut themselves in their room, not coming out to be with the family? Are they disinterested in activities that they used to love, like sports or band? Are they distant from the family pet all of a sudden? Watch for these kinds of behaviors and see if something is bothering them. You may need to search their room to see if there's any evidence that would uncover a problem. Pay attention to new friends who may or may not be good influences on them, and pay attention to what they're listening to. This is a time when kids develop in the area of emotional intelligence; it's critical they have a healthy self-esteem. A positive view of themselves is vital to their well-being.

I know some of this sounds intrusive, but your child's life could be at stake. If you're overly trustworthy, you may be enabling them to indulge in behaviors that can harm them and bring lasting consequences.

As a parent you can intervene by spending time with your teens, asking the right questions, and even subtly interviewing their friends. This may not be easy as a teen can overreact to your interest in them, viewing it as an effort to stifle their independence. These are some reasons why the teen years can be so challenging. I'm going to repeat myself, and I hope you'll hear me. Listen to the hints they give, listen to the tone they use, listen to their cry for attention and affirmation. Do everything you can to build them up and find ways to connect on any level. Walk through, talk through the days, months and years.

Joe

<u>Chores in the Teens Years</u>

My wife contends that the piles of homework children drag home are "parent homework piles," such as when the pile is too much for a fifth grader and the parent has to stay up half the night helping to finish it. Sometimes I feel that way about chores for teenagers. We gave our kids chores and still do. Just because a child is in college doesn't negate their household responsibilities when they come home on break, such as unloading the dishwasher, taking out the trash or cleaning the downstairs bathroom. But getting teens to remember and follow through with their responsibilities often feels as if we're battling teenage-onset dementia. "Hey, the trash is overflowing. Before wild animals break in and nest in there, do you think you might want to take it out?" "Me!? When did you tell me to do that?" "Oh, about 436 times this month. I've kept a log. Care to see it?" The parent homework analogy applies. Enforcement of chores is sometimes work for the parent. Enforcement is worthy work. Enforcement fine-tunes the attitudes. The process sharpens and prepares children for the future.

One tip that is helpful is to make sure the kids are in the right seat as it relates to chores. They are on the right bus—the family bus. If the kid has a propensity toward cleaning, push them in that direction. We have one that cooks. Kennon. Go Kennon. He is good and growing in that direction. If one of your children likes to haggle with the cable company and understands tech, turn 'em loose! One of our kids is gifted at organization. Big picture person. She is adept at turning a big mess into an organized space. Other kids are detail people. The whole house may look like a tornado hit it, but the space between the washer and dryer is immaculate. "Big" overwhelms those personality types. Small and concentrated is what works for them. Not all chores fall into the "personal gift set" mix that brings satisfaction. The word "chore" bespeaks drudgery. The point here is to preclude as much drudgery as possible by assigning certain chores to certain kids in order to help them succeed.

Rules and Discipline

Kids are so different. Coach Phil Jackson, the legendary coach of the Chicago Bulls and Los Angeles Lakers, had several unique leadership philosophies. I have never subscribed to the mystical ones, but there was another of his philosophies I disagreed with at first, then eventually came around to: he treated individual players differently. For example, he wouldn't require the same thing of a Dennis Rodman that he did a Michael Jordan. He would seem to pamper some while publicly deriding others. The thing is, Jackson knew his players and he knew what motivated them. A press conference insult might light a fire in one that would propel the guy to his personal record the next night, while it would devastate another player, sending him into an emotional cave requiring a rescue operation to get him out.

In the same vein, kids are different and unique. Our children look so much alike that even I get them mixed up sometimes if the light isn't just right. Our son Joseph told me when he was in the fifth grade, "I'm going to Southeastern University when I grow up and I'm going to preach the Gospel." To my knowledge he never wavered, never entertained another course. That same child came home from high school one day and said, "I met a girl today. I don't know, Dad, I think she could be the one." Whatever. Whatever! He never wavered. She *was* the one, and that high school sweetheart gave us our first grandchild recently.

Although our children look alike, their motivators are very different. There is a currency to our kids and we have to find out what that currency is. One child might be motivated to work his/her hardest for the currency of, well, currency. When I bring money into the equation for one child, I know I'll get their very best. Money to another one of my kids may be met with a shrug and a "whatever" attitude. It doesn't have the same sizzle. But what motivates that child may be a word of affirmation. "You're an amazing child. Mom and I are very thankful. It will really help us if you change the atmosphere of your room from bombed out Afghanistan to suburban USA."

One of my kids responds to disappointment. If I look downcast and mention softly, "That really lets me down," a tsunami of emotions and repentance will wash over that child. The important thing is to understand and utilize the "currency" of the child without becoming manipulative. Manipulation—even flattery, which the Bible says spreads a net to trap—is never healthy. As Jerry said, there is the day to confront. Sometimes you have to go toe to toe and nose to nose. I've had to do that and it's never fun. As the assistant principal at my high school used to tell those he had to discipline, "Sorry, bud, but you're not allowed to win this. It wouldn't be right." I received that speech just before I received the board of education (a.k.a. the paddle) from Mr. Lewis on one occasion. The inmates cannot run the asylum, as they say. It can't be allowed to happen. The kids have parameters and can run in great freedom but they are not in charge, and in the teenage years, especially, they must have "the way of the Lord explained more perfectly unto them" on occasion.

Jacob Aranza wrote a book I often referred to when I was a youth pastor. It's titled, *Lord! Why is My Child a Rebel?* In the book, there's a description of a prodigal child. The truth that I locked onto is that the rules of the house are set. If the son cannot abide by the rules, they cannot remain. Whenever the prodigal ended up in the pigpen, impoverished and friendless as he inevitably did, the father ran to the reconciliation. However, and this is key, the house rules didn't change. There were established boundaries at the front and the back of the prodigal experience. That truth applies to the discipline of children at your house and mine. These are our boundaries. End of story.

As a former athlete and a fan of athletics, I derive a great many truths and examples from the sports world. I was able to attend a Duke basketball game in my home state of North Carolina. Watching the Duke basketball team is like watching a military marching band, which is not surprising since their coach, Mike Krzyzewski, is a West Point graduate. I was fascinated at the way the team entered Cameron Indoor Stadium and at the precision of the time outs. I even found the way they folded the towels to be fascinating. Duke basketball, love it or hate it, is championship basketball.

Coach Krzyewski has very few rules for his team, as outlined in his book on leadership. Grant Hill played at Duke University for four years under Coach "K." He was a two-time NCAA All-American and a two-time National Champion. He also went on to a very prestigious nineteen seasons in the NBA and was a 1996 Olympic Gold Medal champion for the USA. Grant Hill valued these principles:

- People set rules to keep from making decisions.
- The deal is the handshake. The deal is that there won't be any

deals.

- We have only one rule here: Don't do anything that's detrimental to yourself. Because if it's detrimental to you, it'll be detrimental to our program and to Duke University.

- As the team gathers together in our locker room for the first time, I try to get my only rule out of the way fast. I won't dwell on it because I'd rather not ruin the moment. This is a great day—a day that I've been looking forward to with anxious anticipation for months. You can feel the excitement in the air. You can see the spring in everyone's step.

Raising responsible human beings is different than training basketball players. However, I think Coach K's philosophy is important as it relates to family. The Prodigal's father probably didn't have a policy manual nine inches thick. The boundaries shouldn't be as thick as the menu at a Cheesecake Factory, but while Coach has one rule, we should have a handful. At the Phillips' Crib, it was unity, respect, truth, godliness and not a lot of others. If your boundaries look like the IRS code, enforcement will be a nightmare. The Phillips' code was short but enforced.

Another youth ministry book from the ancient times I read was *10 Mistakes Parents Make with Teenagers*. I remember one great tip from that book. Major on the majors and minor on the minors. A made bed perhaps should have been major, but to me it was minor (except the whole soccer situation previously mentioned). The military makes it major and for good reason, I'm sure. Unity? Unity is major. A house divided will not stand, and I enforced that boundary the entire time we raised our children.

Cecilia and I have utilized essay writing in discipline and child rearing on occasion. A couple of funny essays stand out. One I kept and one I wish I had kept. My daughter Lauren wanted to be baptized when she was seven years old. Baptism is like a pretty big deal being a sacrament and all. It's one of two holy ordinances in Scripture, so I wanted to make sure little Lauren understood the gravity and joy of this decision. I asked her to explain her desire, in writing. She produced the following essay on May 3, 1998. I rewrite it exactly as she put it down on notebook paper:

I Want to be Baptize

Why? because I want to live for Chist and I won't to have him in all that I do and I think God is telling me to do it so I want to do it and I won't to do what is write and what he says.

Lauren Phillips

She printed the essay and wrote in cursive for her signature; she also added two big-eyed smiley faces to help sway the judge's decision. Well, this judge was certainly swayed! That little girl convinced me with her own words that she knew what God was doing in her life.

Another essay comes to mind. I got sick of my older son aggravating the younger one. So, instead of intervening with some great pain and reward paradigm or other parental pronouncement, I made my thirteen-year-old son write an essay about his behavior and attitude toward his seven-year-old sibling. Oh, how I wish I had saved it. I will paraphrase from memory. I do remember a couple of words. Remember that my children didn't have smart phones at the time so I'm not exactly sure where he got this stuff.

I am writing to apologize for my egregious transgression toward the diminutive and innocent child Kennon. My behavior exceeded normal preconscious boundaries and does not reflect the depth of tenderness I feel for this sibling. Nor does my behavior reflect the parameters of God's holy requirements.

The essay was so smart-alecky and absurd that I could do nothing but laugh and let the boy out of the hot seat. College entrance essays have been far less intelligent and flowery.

Connecting with Your Teen

Do special things with your kids as often as possible. Cecilia does individual things with the kids even to this day. Every one of the things we do makes a memory. I do some special things as well and make it a point to deliberately have one intentional "touch" per day with at least one of the kids. Last week I spent an hour and a half with Madeline on the phone while I did some cleaning up around the house. The call had been scheduled for a week. It's good to schedule things in advance. It may seem more professional than personal, but I believe it actually validates the importance of the relationship. Meetings are important. Meetings are scheduled. Doctor appointments are scheduled. Even dinners with friends are scheduled. We have an open-door policy with our kids. Call any time and for anything. However, an appointment provides this promise: "Sugar, when you call, I'll be looking forward to it and you'll have my undivided attention. I may be mopping a floor or folding a towel but that takes very little of my brainpower." Plus, an appointment is something you can look forward to for days.

Lauren and I had a standing appointment for years when she was in elementary school. I picked her up from school every Wednesday and we headed to historic downtown Concord, NC, to the Smelly Cat Coffee Shop. No kidding, that was the name of it. Many of our students fasted every

Wednesday and officially broke the fast at four p.m. Lauren did not fast, but watched her father deliciously break that fast with pastries and ice cream at the Smelly Cat. Then I fine-tuned my sermon and she did homework. The baked goods and ice cream were beyond delicious and we both really enjoyed them. Lauren was precious. She was studious and rarely asked questions while I studied, though we did take breaks to laugh and talk. That is a wonderful memory.

Each family is made up of characters that together create a unique family chemistry and dynamic. In the Philips home, I was Joseph's hero. We were inseparable. When Kennon came along, the natural progression was for Joseph to step into that role for his younger brother, which he did. He became Kennon's hero. I played basketball with them when I could, among other things. Eventually, they crushed me on the court, which is the way all old men go. My knees eventually vetoed basketball as a special activity between us. Enter stage left a new activity: disc golf, which is a game where players throw a Frisbee-like disc at a basket-like target. The object is to get through the course with the fewest number of tosses of the disc. I was introduced to the sport while traveling in Michigan. I was awful to begin with. I even managed to throw the disc behind me a couple of times before I got the hang of it. But I loved it and bought all three of us a pack of discs at the local sporting goods store. The boys enjoyed it so much they started trading discs online. They've played dozens of courses, hundreds of times. Eventually Lauren got in on the deal. All the kids are really good and Dad is getting crushed again, but the knees are grateful. Our family doesn't hunt like Jerry's family. We harbor no religious or ethical reason not to. I just didn't grow up doing that and didn't raise my kids in the sport. There have been times I've regretted it. However, we do hunt discs that go off the path into the woods. Does that count? I mean, the kids and I are in the woods crunching leaves under foot. Together. Crisp air. Challenge of a good shot. Talking about it after the fact. Those are special moments.

Nine years ago when we moved back to North Carolina, I spent a few years at the kids' school teaching a Bible class. I wanted them to have the best Christian education I could find. Our great headmaster, Frank Cantadore, provided an opportunity for me to teach when I wasn't traveling so that my children could attend the school. The youngest three graduated from there. The reader may not have the opportunity to do something like that, but it was clutch for us. I wasn't in the children's business at school *too* much. At least I tried not to be. I did get to see their faces daily and I was there when they needed anything. It was tough to work forty-five hours per week in exchange for their education, but it was worth it and I have no regrets about it.

Funding the Fun for Your Teen

We funded a lot of stuff, and said no to a lot of stuff. That's about it. We provided opportunities for our kids to earn money for activities they wanted to participate in. Sometimes it was our pleasure to bless them with the funds they needed for things such as missions trips. Missions trips are important for a variety of reasons. One reason is the *process*. Part of the process is having or developing the faith for finances. We helped to a point, but we encouraged our children in the process that was established by the sending organization of raising the money needed for the trip.

My son was fourteen and working at a grocery store. He had a girlfriend from middle school. She lived inside a gated home. Not a gated community. A mansion with a gate. Needless to say, her life experience was vastly different from my son's life experience regarding finances, privilege and opportunity. When it came time for his Valentine's date, I was about as interested in funding his love life as my own father would have been to fund mine. Joseph was making money. He was enrolled in the best private school we could afford and we were meeting his needs, so it was time for him to learn and grow. His reporting of the date went something like this: "She ordered an appetizer. She barely ate it. She ordered an expensive meal. Barely ate it. Ordered a drink and dessert and picked at the dessert." Then they walked across the parking lot and he bought two movie tickets. "Dad, she ordered the biggest bucket of popcorn and the most expensive candy." When my son discovered how expensive love could be, the shine was off the apple. That was their last date. Money talks. Sometimes it tells people—young and old—about what is valuable.

On this subject I feel a little like the parent that says, "Do as I say and not as I do." As a great mentor of mine once answered during a Q & A when asked about his physical exercise regimen, "There is a limit to my hypocrisy." The man was a genius in a plethora of subjects. Fitness, not so much. I am not an expert at much. I do know what I am not an expert at. Funding the fun in teenagers is that. Regarding this topic, my advice is perhaps: take my friend Jerry's advice and also ask some others.

The Dating Game

I'm going to pick on Lauren and her childhood preciousness a little longer. I can still see her sitting in a little rocking chair on a particular Sunday afternoon. She was six or seven years old. In those days we had three morning services at our church, followed by lunch and a brief nap, then back to church for Sunday night service. Little Lauren had worn a short, purple skirt and thick purple tights that morning. We were close to loading up for the evening service and I noticed that she was wearing the same outfit but wasn't wearing the tights. For reasons I can't remember, I playfully said, "Lauren, you're not wearing the tights tonight? You little vixen." Without missing a beat, Lauren looked at me and maturely, if not authoritatively, answered, "Who you calling a vixen, you little pervit?" What an insult! She was aiming at "pervert" (who knows what movie or teenager she picked that up from) but she landed on "pervit." Pervit, of course, made it into the Phillips' Family Lexicon. We all know the backstory as we shoot it as an insult to something or somebody.

We have always had an open-door policy with our kids; anything was and is open for discussion. I'm grateful that was the way we did things. I always wanted our children to get their sex education from home and not the neighborhood, school or some other "concerned" adult that wasn't their mom or dad. Joseph and I have always been very close. He has always had an inquisitive mind. So early on, I matter-of-factly instructed him on the facts of life in an age-appropriate way. He got the important information about girls from his parents.

For the other three children I got a good idea, as memory allows, from Dr. James Dobson. I admit it could have been from a random radio program or other place. When Lauren was thirteen, I took her with me to New York, where I had to go for a ministry trip in Brooklyn. We stayed in Queens and made reservations at Tavern on the Green in Central Park. We really dressed up that evening. She wore a beautiful dress and I was in a suit and tie. It was my intention to inform Lauren about the facts of life on this trip. I really liked the idea of having "the talk" at an iconic place like New York City. So many television shows and movies have New York as a backdrop. I wanted her to constantly, if not subconsciously, make the connection between New York City and what she learned about holiness and the joy of intimacy. An old historic restaurant like Tavern on the Green just added to the mystique. I admit I was more nervous telling my oldest daughter about the birds and the bees than if I had been speaking to an audience of thousands. I was so nervous, in fact, that I called my wife so we could pray together. I went to the restaurant gift shop to buy Lauren a gift. Later I called the manager of the restaurant over to the table and introduced myself and Lauren to him. I asked him if famous people still frequented the place. In a very thick New York accent he said, "Whattaya talkin' about?! Who you want? Politics? Movie stars? Last night, Halle Barry sat right there. Two days ago, Clint Eastwood right next to you over here." He mentioned a few others. We were both very impressed. After a wonderful meal, it was time for the "business" portion of the evening. I proceeded to tell Lauren about dating. The anatomical differences between genders. I talked about responses, defrauding, appropriate touching and *in*appropriate touching. Lauren listened. Finally when I had finished the lecture I looked at my timid little darling and asked, "Do you have any questions? Anything is fair game." She said quietly, "Just one Daddy." "What is it, baby doll?" "Can we talk about something else?" I sighed a tremendous sigh and said, "Sure, sweetie. Let's get dessert. But just one more thing." I passed her gift across the table. It was a beautiful ornamental gold bag inside a Tavern-on-the-Green gift bag. I said, "This little gift bag represents your purity. I want you to put this in your room where you can see it. Remember that it's a symbol of your purity. I want you to give this to your husband on your wedding night. Tell him, 'I've been saving this for many years, long before I met you, so that I could give it to you tonight. It represents my chastity and purity. I've been kept by God for this very night.'" Lauren still has that gift for her future husband in a place she can look at often.

One funny thing that happened in connection with this happened with my youngest daughter, Madeline. Because she and Kennon are only eighteen months apart in age, I decided to do a "two-fer," taking them both to New York at the same time for "the talk." Tavern on the Green was closed so we ended up at a much-less-extravagant spot in Times Square: a sidewalk pizza place. I gave them both the speech—and saved the expense of another trip to New York, New York, and gave them their symbolic gifts to present to their mates on their wedding nights. When I finished the talk, nervous but somehow far less than I had been with Lauren, I asked if there were any questions. Kennon was a little fidgety, but receptive. He had no questions. They knew what the meeting entailed. Lauren had prepared them. But Madeline said, "I have some," and she pulled out a piece of paper with a long list of questions! And they were specific! We plodded through the items on the list, one by one, really putting my open-door policy to the test. We got through it and I continue to have an open door policy ... and Madeline has continued to open the door!

Joseph dated one girl. He eventually married her. Kennon has dated a few, casually, and one rather seriously as of this writing. Lauren has a very high bar regarding her future husband and I'm grateful she does. She is stunning, and waiting for God's perfect will. She didn't casually date in high school. Madeline had a couple of casual dates. She is equally stunning and equally waiting for God's will.

When I'm doing a comedy routine, I run through a list of maladies that come with old age. The usual stuff: knees, unwanted eyebrow hair, frequent trips in the night to the restroom and such. I talk about having to go to a specialist a few years ago when I thought I was having a heart attack. "I walked into the waiting room of the specialist and thought, 'Look at these people; how much time do I have?'" is how the comedy bit begins. Then I talk about the long, rather personal, medical questionnaire that they gave me to fill out. The bright spot of going through the trauma of seeing a specialist (by the way it wasn't my heart, rather a reflux diagnosis, which is a frequent diagnosis for those who fear an impending widow-maker heart attack) was this questionnaire. Total strangers expected me to give very personal information on that form. Logic told me I would see those same people at the mall in the future.

That questionnaire got me thinking. Whenever a hairy-legged boy comes to my house to pick up my daughter for a date, I will be ready. I decided to offer them an information acquisition tool. Here are a few of the actual questions from the medical form that I have borrowed and am prepared to share with prospective boyfriends:

1. Have you ever had a contagious disease?
2. Do you use snuff?
3. Do you drink alcohol?
4. Are you having any angina, chest pain?
5. Shortness of breath?
6. Emotional/psychiatric problems?
7. Nausea/vomiting x 3 days?
8. Diarrhea or "coffee grounds?" (*Don't worry, son, if you don't know what that is. If you had it, you'd know it!*)
9. Change of bowel habits?
10. Paralysis?
11. Amputation? (*Son, here is a follow-up question of my own. If you were to have an amputation, where would you prefer it?*)
12. Is there a church/minister you'd like us to notify?
13. Do you feel positive about your ability to deal with hospitalization?

    My daughter: "*Dad, come on!*"

    Me: "*Hush your mouth. Total strangers wanted me to answer these questions. This boy wants to put you in a thousand-pound truck and drive you on a date. I need to know some things.*"
14. Do you feel unsafe at home? (*Here is another follow-up of mine.*

Do you feel unsafe in this home?)

15. Finally, do you have a living will?

Not many fathers can say they watched their daughters get one of their first kisses, along with hundreds of other people watching! That is, unless they launched some kind of spyware equipment into the date. I had the very odd experience of witnessing just that. My daughter won the lead in the school play, *Annie Get Your Gun,* her senior year of high school. A young man named Jackson laid one on her in every performance. No little peck on the cheek either. I have video and photographic evidence. Madeline said some ladies yelled, "O, Lawd!" I-not-so-affectionately referred to this boy as "Action Jackson." I wish I could capture in words the look on his face in the lobby after the show when I yelled, "Hey, buddy! That's my little girl you're accosting on that stage!" He blinked a few times, trying to find an adequate response. Then I stepped close to him with a smile and a pat on the shoulder. "Great performance. I'm really proud of you both," I said, effectually letting him off the hook.

Cars & Drivers' Licenses

God desires individuals to be independent, interdependent and able to exercise free will, becoming responsible adults. Part of that process is for children to have transportation options. Unless you're reading this in New York City and your only transportation need is a subway card, driving is very important. Like most parents, we encouraged, supported and provided opportunities for our kids to drive. They all got their licenses on the first or second try.

God has provided vehicles for us for years. I'm fifty-one as of this writing. I've never owned a new car. Before hard times hit our family in my childhood, I remember my dad drove company cars that had that "new car smell." My kids have no such memory. But God has brought a great many vehicles to us. One of my favorite memories is our Lauren praying for a vehicle when she was a junior in high school. It really isn't cool to be dropped off at school in your folk's minivan when you're a junior in high school, but she had a great attitude about it, or at least I thought so. She recently told me she was perplexed that the most heathen kids had the nicest cars. Then, one night after church she told the Lord, "I'm not entitled to a car. If You choose to bless me, it will not be because I deserve it. It will be because I am your daughter." Two days later a friend of Cecilia's asked her what kind of car Lauren had. She told the sweet lady, "Lauren is believing God for a vehicle." Cecilia's friend responded something like, "Good. We have an extra one in the shop we would like to donate to the ministry." We told Lauren to meet us that night at a local fast food place. We made sure her friend Haley, who was in on the surprise, got her there on time. Lauren said, "Dad, thanks for dropping off the van, but we need to be quick about this meal. I need to get to Wednesday night church." She hurried me along about three times. Finally, I said, "Okay. Let's go out and get Mom's van. Just follow me." We walked out to the parking lot. I had parked the old van out of sight by the dumpster. "Where is the van, Dad?" Lauren asked. "I need to get to church." I looked left and right and said, "I don't know, just take that car." I pointed to the red car she didn't know was hers yet. "Real funny, Dad. Come on, I don't want to be late. Where's the van?" I pulled out the keys and hit the unlock button and said, "Since you're in a hurry just take that one." "Is it one of your rental cars?" she asked. At the time even I didn't have a decent car and had to rent cars for every road trip. "Honey," I said, "that isn't a rental car. That's the answer to your prayer. That car is yours." That moment is captured in my mind forever. I had never seen a person laugh and cry at the exact same instant. Lauren did. Gut laughs and snotty wails. It was a precious testament to her about the power of her prayers and the faithfulness of God.

God provided in similar ways for Joseph and Madeline. Their grandparents gave them older but reliable vehicles. Kennon worked in a yogurt shop and saved his money. He is our entrepreneur. He paid cash for a reliable car. A few months later he was driving to a church beach retreat and he flipped the car when the right tire went off the road and he overcompensated. Cecilia and I were paying liability insurance and so all the money he had earned and saved for the car was lost. I told Kennon in the hospital (what a great miracle Kennon was: two small broken bones in his hands and some striped scars on his arm) that the Lord would make a way to replace his car. I guaranteed it. God provided me $2,000 a few weeks later, which I used to replace what Kennon lost. So just *days* after the accident, I gave Kennon the money as a graduation and birthday gift—both dates in May. I'll never forget two things about that gift. I have this first unforgettable aspect on video. When I presented him the money he said, "Wow, you're a man of your word, Dad." The other thing I remember is that before I gave him the money, I brought the other three kids into our bedroom and told them what I had in mind. I asked them if they thought that was unfair because I wasn't able to do the same things for them. They looked at me, stunned. I thought they were processing what I had just told them I wanted to do. Rather, they were stunned at what they considered the ludicrous nature of the question. It was a no-brainer. "We celebrate each other's good fortune." "We think that's awesome." "Of course we don't care, Dad." I was really proud of the kids that day.

CHAPTER 6

PREPARING YOUR CHILDREN
FOR ADULTHOOD

Jerry

The process of preparing your kids for leaving home is an interesting one. We all want our kids to make the right choices in schools, friends, jobs and mates. This process begins in your home the last few years they are with you. It is a learning time for your child in facing the real world. They may work for a boss who does not encourage or support, or who is cruel or demanding without reasonable expectations. This is tough, but it's the real world. They may meet someone who breaks their heart, and this too is the real world. They may have professors at school who challenge the values they've been taught, and they will have to choose for themselves what to believe.

As parents we are listeners, encouragers, coaches, and counselors. How we respond and encourage our kids is critical during this time in their lives. They may not always listen to good advice and will pay the consequences as a result. Avoid saying, "I told you so," if this happens. They are becoming adults, which is never an easy process.

Family Values

Every family has values, some good and some bad. The values you live by in your home are the operational values that your kids will learn and adapt to. You can say you have certain values at church or in the community, but if you don't live them at home, your "values" are nothing more than a pipe dream. Your kids know better. What you consistently do defines your values.

Do you value time with your family? Do you value each other's space and not provoke one another just for the fun of it? Who does the cleaning, cooking and yard work? Who decorates the Christmas tree and buys the gifts for birthdays? Do you respect one another? Do you respect others? Are you honest? Do you steal? Who is responsible to buy the groceries, do the laundry, or help the kids with homework? Who changes the dirty diapers? Who takes the kids to practice for band, football, soccer, youth group and other activities? If the bulk of responsibility falls on one person, there are likely some values out of line. Some believe they work hard at the office and don't have to do any of these things at home. I suggest that all of these chores, no matter who works outside the home and who doesn't, should be shared chores and responsibilities.

How we treat one another, how we talk to one another, even our facial expressions communicate values in our home. Listen, selfishness is rampant in this generation and people all want "their" time. But when we have a family and rent or own a home, we have responsibilities that require more from us. We can't just do what we want, when we want, if we are married, have kids and hope to raise a functional family. Grow up! Turn the TV off! Turn your cell phone off! Become a servant leader in your home and go the extra mile. Be a "second miler." A marriage where there is at least one second miler is a stronger marriage, and strong families emerge from "second-miler" homes. When you are willing to go the second mile to help your family, to serve your mate or assure your child is safe, whole and fed, you will see results. These are values.

Libby and I made it a point to teach our values to our kids from an early age. Some of the values we focused on were love for God and love for one another, faith, respect, honesty, generosity in giving, forgiveness, and a strong work ethic. With God's help we did our best to model those values to our children. I believe we should model the life of Christ to our children rather than just preach it to them. In real life we must be role models and let our lives do more talking than our mouths. We weren't preachy to our kids. Instead, we tried to live the life of an authentic Christian in front of them. No, we weren't perfect, and yes we taught the kids forgiveness by asking them to forgive us when we got angry with them or didn't respond as we should have when someone cut us off in traffic.

We live out what we believe in front of our kids, who see us at our best and worst. What values do we project when we are hurting, angry, upset, under stress and under financial pressure? We all live in a real world, with real world problems, and these stressors get to us all at some level. How we behave at such times are the messages we send and the values we project to our kids, and those are the values they will ultimately embrace for themselves.

We taught our children to have faith in God and His unending love since they were very young. We prayed together as a family for our needs and the needs of others, and we read the Bible together. We taught our kids respect for one another and for their elders. We taught them to say "Yes, sir" and "Yes, ma'am" to adults. We taught them to respect each other's toys and property, and not to "borrow" without asking. We also taught them the importance of honesty. It's essential in every part of our lives and plays a huge role in who we are and who we become. Integrity is everything. I believe values are more *caught* than *taught*, so give that some thought as you consider how you can best serve your family.

These are things we taught our children in preparation for adulthood.

Leadership Training

As you assign chores to your children, work on projects together, or spend time in the car together, you are training them. Whether you realize it or not, every moment you spend with your child is a training opportunity. An important aspect of that training is in the area of leadership. Talk about your work with your children and how you solve problems that arise. My kids loved coming to work with me when they were young. They liked seeing my office, and they especially liked helping with some of my work activities. This gave me opportunities to instill leadership principles into them as they grew into young adults.

When Libby and I took the President/CEO role in Teen Challenge in 1991, we started doing staff training with our team. We felt it was one of the most critical parts of establishing a baseline among our team for future growth. We took one day a month to meet with them, pray with them, and teach them leadership principles. We brought that conviction home and shared concepts along the way with our kids. We didn't force leadership lessons on them, but imparted them casually as we lived life together, passing along principles in the process. It might be in the process of shopping for their first car, or discussing what college they should go to, or helping them through a life crisis. Those were all leadership training opportunities.

One friend of mine told me he would pay his kids to read books. He would give them books on leadership, history and other thought-provoking materials and pay them for completing what he assigned. I wish I had thought of that with my kids, and that my parents had thought of that with me.

First Jobs

It was interesting when my kids began to get jobs. I wanted them to work and learn how to be in a new environment where they needed to perform and achieve at something totally unfamiliar to them. I was proud the day each of them secured jobs on their own, even if it was in a fast-food restaurant. Two of my three children worked at Chick-fil-A and they loved the environment and work experience. The store's values were similar to the values our children learned at home and they seemed to enjoy the people they worked with as well as the customers. They were now responsible to put in a certain number of hours each week and would get paid for the first time from outside the family.

I can't express how excited each of them was when they got their first pay check. They saw the numbers on an official company check that had their name on it. The check represented a value to them. They had worked and were being reimbursed for their time and effort. I believe this is a healthy experience for kids and suggest you give your child a chance to work in something other than the family business. It opens their eyes to another reality that will help them down the road.

Submitting to and Respecting Authority

One of the things we tried to teach our kids, as well as the young people we mentored, was to develop a healthy respect for authority. We wanted our kids to respect the people they worked for. This seems easy to teach in theory, but real life can offer some amazing challenges, because as we all know, there are all kinds of leaders. From the outside some pastors and business and ministry leaders look like they have it all together and that they would be great people to work for. We all know that's not always true, which creates a risk every time you change jobs or workplaces. I have a saying, "If the grass is greener on the other side of the fence, it's generally because there's more manure." Jumping ship and changing jobs every time one faces a challenge is not a good idea. Lessons are better learned by staying the course and growing through adversity.

I think many of us have gone to work for someone hoping it would be our dream job, only to find it's more of a nightmare. I always told my kids to respect authority even if they didn't believe in everything their employer stood for or their management style. I taught them that God expects us to submit to those in authority and that He will honor us if we do. And I also taught them the importance of loyalty and of not speaking ill of the leader. This is one of the most important lessons they can learn.

I believe there's a lot you can learn by keeping your mouth shut, then praying and letting God lead you to the next step on your journey. If you quit out of frustration or run from a challenging personality, you will likely get another chance to learn that lesson later on down the road.

Our kids need to learn to bloom where they're planted. They need to learn to keep a good attitude in all situations. That doesn't mean they have to practice every activity or attitude of the leader they are serving. Like us, they need to learn to chew the meat and spit out the bones. But a parent should not protect their kids from the hard lessons of life. That can be a challenge for me because I'm a problem solver. I do it all day, every day. But the best thing I can do for my teenage child is to allow him or her to learn how to deal with problems. I want to be there to listen and guide, but there comes a time when they have to learn how to solve their own problems. I don't do them any favors by doing it for them.

Exposing Your Kids to Conversations with Adults

From the time our children were young, Libby and I included them in many of our conversations. We also liked to include them in conversations we had with other adults. We often had international guests in our home and at night we would spend hours talking. Our kids enjoyed sitting in the living room with us, listening to the conversations. We encouraged them to ask questions to learn about other cultures and other people's positions on issues. They always seemed to enjoy hearing the accents, the stories, and getting to know Teen Challenge leaders from around the world. These conversations broadened their minds and made them comfortable speaking to adults.

As kids, my twin brother and I worked in our dad's shoe store, stocking shelves, organizing shoes, vacuuming and dusting. When the store got busy my dad would ask me to help customers find shoes and then he would come by when he was free to check the sizes with the customer. From the age of twelve, I began speaking to adults about shoes. It increased my comfort level in speaking to people older than me. I didn't realize then how beneficial those conversations were for my development. It taught me how important it is for children to interact with adults other than their parents in order to develop a healthy view of people and a comfort level in conversing with adults.

Teaching Stewardship

The principle of giving is best taught from parents. Yes, our kids will hear teaching at church on the practice of giving, but we need to be their role models. My dad and mom taught me to give as a child. When I was five years old I received fifteen cents a week for doing chores. The chores were simple, like making my bed, cleaning my room, feeding the dog, and other things a five-year-old child could do.

When I got my allowance, I was taught to put five cents in a mason jar, which served as my piggy bank and was for saving. I put another five cents in the Sunday school offering. And the final five cents was mine to spend as I wanted. My brother and I would run to the store, each with a nickel in our pockets, to buy gum and candy. We'd come home with our pockets full and we'd make it last all week. We followed that routine every week when we got our fifteen cents.

My brother and I had lawn-mowing jobs at the age of ten and made money doing other odd jobs around the neighborhood. My parents taught us to pay ten percent on everything we made. I was very excited when my dad took me to the bank and helped me open my first bank account. I'll never forget learning how to write a check to pay for something. I saved up and paid cash for my first motorcycle. I learned how to appreciate watching the amounts in my savings account grow, and it helped me not spend everything I earned on unnecessary things. I left for college with several thousand dollars in my savings account and actually graduated college with about the same amount in savings.

Libby and I taught our kids to give and to be generous when they gave. I'll never forget one night in December when the Toys for Tots volunteers knocked on our door. Our kids were all under the age of ten, and when they heard the volunteers ask for used toys to give to kids who were less fortunate for Christmas, they ran to their closets and came back with some of their best toys to donate. I cringed when they brought their most expensive toys to give away. I even asked if they were sure that's what they wanted to do. But I was also proud they didn't want to give their old toys, but their new ones. We allowed it with a bit of hesitation, but we were proud of our kids' generosity. They were heroes to me.

Extended Missions Trips

We always supported our kids going on missions trips with the church youth group. We felt the more they were exposed to other countries and cultures, the better view of life they would have. American kids can be very self-centered and materialistic, but that can change when they're exposed to the needs of those less fortunate at home and abroad. Our kids always came home from missions trips with a burden for those they had met and those who were in need.

We encouraged them to take at least one extended missions trip alone, without their friends, to a country of their choice. And we also encouraged them to consider an internship at one of the Teen Challenge centers around the world. Our oldest daughter Denee' went to Cebu City, Philippines, and it was a life-changing experience. She went down into caves where poor families were living because they couldn't afford anything more. Denee' spoke of the smell of urine and waste which made her sick to her stomach. She saw kids living in the back of a cemetery, playing among the bones of human skeletons that were taken from the tombs of the families who could no longer pay for the annual maintenance fee. She went to college with a much broader picture of the world and of human need. As a result, she continues to be generous and caring of others.

Kristi went to Portugal and served with the Teen Challenge team there. She assisted with the women's home and did whatever she was asked to do. She came to love the staff and students in the program. Her mid-afternoon coffees with the staff were highlights of her days. She fit into the culture well and came to appreciate Portugal and the wonderful people of that country. She was exposed to the hurting, and it changed her life.

Dustin went to the Czech Republic as well as Portugal. He had finished his classes early in his senior year so he spent three months between those two countries. He spent a lot of time with Petr' Minister, the director of Teen Challenge in the Czech Republic, and came to love the Czech people. He did everything from painting stairwells to driving the Executive Director around the country. He learned to serve and give of himself with a limited number of English-speaking people around, and came home speaking enough Czech to be sassy in that beautiful language.

These and other experiences prepared our children for the transition from home to college, to careers and to marriage. We are extremely proud of each of our children.

Joe

Family Values

We have a few values that are critical in our home. Here is a list that is neither in order of importance nor comprehensive.

Hospitality

I shared in the Holiday section about the importance of opening our home to others. Hospitality. That is indeed a value. In Huntington, West Virginia, there is a beautiful little university called Marshall. The film *We Are Marshall* brought worldwide attention to it. We were living there when they made the movie, which is pretty cool. Marshall has a large population of international students within the student body. Someone from the university called me when I was the pastor of a church in town. The local newspaper had done a story about a young woman from Spain named Rosio (pronounced Ro-the'-o). The article spoke of her loneliness as everyone went home at Christmas and she was left to wander the dormitories alone. They asked me if I would be willing to take her into my home for Easter. My wife was juggling some health challenges at the time. I told her about the call and that I was reluctant to invite this young woman to be with us because of Cecilia's health. We agreed to pray about it and Cecilia told me a few days later she felt the Lord wanted us to open our home to her. Rosio was a Catholic. She smoked. Without even asking her to, she was respectful enough to smoke outside of our house. She went to church every time we did, and we go a lot. She was a very courteous guest in every way. I can't say with an ounce of authenticity that she received the Lord as her Savior because she stayed in our home. I can say that she felt Him and the love of God in our home. We maintain friendly contact with her all these years later. In fact, Lauren spent time with her in Spain not long ago as she opened *her* home to a Phillips.

The Rosio experience actually jump-started a new program in our church, Bethel Temple. We discovered there were lots of Rosios at Marshall. The newspaper did a follow-up story on her with Cecilia and me seated beside Rosio at the famous Marshall fountain (the same one featured in the movie *We Are Marshall,* with Matthew McConaughey). The news article reflected the love she experienced in the home of the Phillips family during the holidays. We later hosted girls from Columbia. We hosted the girls for the Thanksgiving holiday one year. Joining the girls was a student from Turkey (on Turkey Day) and a neighborhood boy about ten years old. During the meal, the young boy started asking the Turkish student about his country. Innocuous questions at first. "Do they have pizza in Turkey?" "What's the weather like?" "Do they play football?" The MU student was happy to answer in English, which was not perfect but pretty good. Then the boy, who was Baptist, asked, "What's your religion?" The Turkish student said, "Most people I know are Muslim." Then the table talk took an awkward and unfortunate turn. "Did you do 9/11?" the boy asked. I had to step in as referee and assure the boy no terrorists were afoot and that he should let our new friend eat. Now pass the potatoes.

Truth

We taught our children as they were growing up that we could get around just about anything but a lie. We told them, "If you do something horrible, face it. Own it. Tell it. We will figure out the consequences and possible solutions." Lies are like water on a table. It runs everywhere, and just when you think it's corralled, it squirts another direction. Lies are Satanic, because Satan is the author of all lies. We put a premium on the truth. Rotten things happen in life and even in ministry when people lie. I remember one awful such occasion. Cecilia and I were always protective of the kids, but not at the expense of this high value: truth. We called the kids into the den and told them the bad situation. We told them the truth minus venom. All the truth included: God knows. God cares. God loves. God promises. We love. We forgive. We press on to the high calling. All God's people gonna be alright. Tell your kids to tell the truth. It really does set us free just like Jesus said it would.

Celebration

Yes, celebration is a value. I spend very little money on trinkets or souvenirs when I travel. Therefore, I've never spent a lot of time looking for just the right thing. Instead, I've taken the money I would have spent on trinkets and used it for celebrations. "Daddy's home!" celebrations. "God did some great work at Daddy's meeting!" celebrations. "Souls saved!" celebrations. I was raised by wonderful, adoptive parents, and for years Dad left on Monday morning and came home on Friday afternoon, so I knew what it felt like for our family to have me away. My travel was never as extensive as my dad's had been, but I still missed a few things I'd rather not have missed. Ordinary stuff. Homework and such. So we loved those Mexican-restaurant celebrations. Or, if the offering was especially good, we enjoyed the steak house or nice Italian restaurant celebrations.

Unity

I demand unity in ministry. I first demand it at home. I take very seriously the words in red: "*If a house is divided against itself, that house cannot stand*" (Mark 3:25, MEV). Since I first heard at Vacation Bible School the story of the house of straw and the house of bricks, I have determined to have a house that withstands the wind. Discord, strife, arguing, enmity, factions, grudges, unforgiveness, retaliation, strife and all such things tear a house down. Conflict is inevitable in relationships. In every institution there will be conflict. My family realized that at some point, unresolved conflict would be met with this admonition from this dad: "Fix it or I will fix it." Having the situation "fixed" by Dad a couple of times was pure incentive for our kids to fix the conflict themselves.

Sharing

A friend of mine once preached there is a difference between giving and sharing. I had not thought of it before, but it is exactly true. I consider each member of our family to be givers. Most of the time I would rather give than share. The obvious example that comes to mind is dessert. If you're eating dessert and a spouse or child asks for a "bite" and proceeds to eat half, you may relate to what I'm saying. "I'd be happy to buy you one!" I might tell them. "You said you didn't want one, but you want to eat mine. I do want one which is why I ordered it." Sharing is important to living together. Cecilia hammered it into the kids' minds early on with a sing-songy declaration: "We're sharers." The previously-mentioned example of the replacement money for Kennon's wreck was a manifestation of this reinforced value.

Encouragement

We wanted to raise a tribe of Barnabas-type people. We wanted "sons (and daughters) of encouragement." Certainly we joked around, picked at and "janked" (a South Georgia word for good-natured denigration) on each other.

When a line was crossed we highlighted the line. Here is the line. Apologize. Uplift each other. Fiercely defend and encourage one another. Technology provides opportunities to encourage like never before. We have a family text thread. Pictures are met with affirmations. "Beautiful." "Cool opportunity." "I love you all." Encouragement is valuable.

Evangelism

My father-in-law, Jimmy Griggs, was a retired postman and an iconic soul-winner in southwest Georgia. The evangelistic fervor he had jumped onto Cecilia. Another treasured memory I have is Cecilia's passion for an old man in Georgia named Mr. McGrail. She was grocery shopping one day and felt a very strong tug of the Holy Spirit about an old man shopping at the same time. She sort of "stalked him" with whatever kids were with her. They were curious about her odd movements and behavior. "The Lord wants us to talk to him," she told them. She obeyed and introduced herself and the kids to him, and exchanged contact information with him. That encounter ultimately led to a friendship between them. Cecilia would take the kids by to see him. He was a very intelligent, former professor at a state university. He was not a believer, but he left this earth with a clear understanding of the Gospel, courtesy of Cecilia Griggs Phillips, which she shared in the presence of the Phillips children. Regular prayer for his salvation undergirded this value. Each of the children care about the souls of people and the importance of sharing the Gospel.

Respect

We expected the kids to respect each other's opinions, property, esteem, sleep and everything else. That meant Cecilia and I had to model respect for each other and for the children too. Regarding their property, we tried to always respect the teenagers' privacy. The caveat was that everybody knew the carte blanche addendum to that policy. Mom and Dad can search the premises any time and without any warning. Your stuff. Our house and our rules.

Leadership Training

Prayer. That is a great leadership tool. Cecilia and I utilized the tool of prayer to train our children. Our styles were definitely different. I joke that when Mom prayed, it was time to tabernacle in the wilderness. Her prayers were detailed and thorough. Her prayers were prayers-to-build-a-fire-for-the-sacrifice prayers. I exaggerate, of course. Mom is a detail person. Dad is a big-picture person. But I truly tried to be faithful in prayer too. When I prayed, it was on-the-fly prayers. I prayed driving to school every day, including the prayer of Jabez. If you're not familiar with the prayer of Jabez, you'll find it in 1 Chronicles 4:10: *"Then Jabez called on the God of Israel, saying, 'Oh, that You would indeed bless me and enlarge my territory, that Your hand might be with me, and that You would keep me from evil, that it may not bring me hardship!' So God granted what he asked."* His prayer included three components:

1. Enlarge our territory, Lord
2. Keep your hand upon us, Lord
3. Keep us from the evil one, Lord

My version of that prayer evolved into this: "Lord, bless us indeed with the big blessings of heaven. Enlarge the border of our influence, Lord. Fill us with the Holy Spirit and keep the devil away from us. We plead the blood over … (then we would pray for each person by name and for their future spouses and children as well, whoever they might be)." To change it up I would occasionally pray the Lord's Prayer, and actually, there are similarities between the two. On one occasion we were unexpectedly given a leather couch and my young son Kennon said, "Dad, this came from the prayer, didn't it? This is one of the big blessings of heaven, right?" I really couldn't argue with that.

Another good technique involving prayer and leadership training is to model immediacy in front of the kids. If you're on the phone, driving with the family, and someone asks you to pray for their wife's health, here is a good thing to do, and it will only take thirty seconds. Tell the man on the phone that you sure will be in prayer for her and hang up. Say to the family, "Hey, kids, that was my friend Bob. His wife is in tough shape. I promised to pray. Let's do that now." Then pray. It will help Bob's wife, which will help Bob. It will also make an impression on the kids and validate the power of prayer and relationship. My father-in-law used to say, "Joe, when I pray for you, two good things happen. First, God helps you when He answers my prayer. And second, I get closer to God as I talk to Him."

There are certain phrases that made their way into the family lexicon. Cecilia would tell the kids as they walked out the door: "Be a blessing." The kids still say that to each other with a smile. More than mockingly saying it, it seems like a tribute to their mother. However they say it and mean it, it certainly is a tribute.

The following is an excerpt from a sermon I wrote called "The Church that Meets at My House."

> Kennon was twelve years old, and having a difficult time
> with the most recent move the day before he was to start at a
> new school. Traveling so much that summer combined with
> his uneasiness of school and the fact that his hero brother,
> Joseph, just left the nest made for some very challenging

days. The night before school was to start he said something to the effect of: "I hate this. I don't want to live here. Everything here is stupid!" We validated his feelings by not *in*validating them. We didn't say, "That's the wrong way to think. Grow up! Don't be selfish." We said nothing like that. Instead, we said a prayer for him and told him we loved him. Kennon went to bed that night, but before long he jumped up and told his sisters, "I need a Bible now." Soon after, he ran into our room very excited. A different young man than the one we said goodnight to excitedly reported on something that had just occurred. "Dad, something really cool just happened. I was in bed and all of a sudden I just knew that I had to look up 2 Corinthians 3:12." Now, here I need to say that Kennon was a good boy, but was more Biblically challenged than the others because he spent more time in public school during his formative years and did not participate in Bible Quiz like his younger sister. He was probably the least likely of the four to have an occurrence like he described that night. "So I didn't have a Bible unpacked in my room yet and I ran into Sissy's room and told her I had to have a Bible. God told me to look up that Bible verse and this is what it says: '*Since this new way gives us such confidence, we can be very bold*'" (2 Corinthians 3:12, NLT). The verse is captured like this only in the version that his sister handed him. I told Kennon that he had just gotten a word from God. I said, "Son, God just communicated a very specific message to you." That particular summer we had seen limbs stretch before our very eyes at an altar in Georgia; a girl with

158 | FUNdamentals in Family Life

cerebral palsy began to walk differently and actually keep up with her siblings in West Virginia; in northern Michigan, we witnessed tumors all over a girl's back shrink (the healing was validated and recently confirmed with the girl in person; they have not grown back). But of everything spiritual and exciting that happened that summer, the most exciting thing that happened to me was my child reporting, "I knew I had to look up that verse." The reason is because it happened at the church that meets at my house.

Here is a metaphor I apply to raising children. Raising kids is almost akin to watching a child playing ball out on a field of play. Imagine a parent standing with their hands on top of a waist-high, chain-link fence. The child has to play the game himself/herself. They have to make the decisions and execute the plays. It's the child's responsibility to exert the energy and hustle required to win the contest. But if something stupid or dangerous happens, the parents are available to jump over the fence and intervene. By stupid, I mean a child being attacked by a parent, the entire opposing team stomping on the child, the referee shoving your child, or the child having a health crisis. That's how Cecilia and I try to parent. We stand with our hands on the chain-link fence. Things that are important but not crucial have to just "play out." A child spends his little paycheck on video games and then needs money for the homecoming formal. Oh well, that was a "bad move" and an L in the win/loss column. When a child has a close relationship that is toxic, like really toxic, then it's time to jump the fence. Addiction? Fence-jumping time.

Parenting from behind a waist-high, chain-link fence is far more effective than being a "helicopter parent." That term was first used in Dr. Haim Ginott's 1969 book, *Parents & Teenagers*, when teenagers he counseled complained that their parents would hover over them like a helicopter. In 2011, the term became popular enough to become a dictionary entry. Ann Dunnewold, Ph. D., a licensed psychologist, calls it "over-parenting." She says, "It means being involved in a child's life in a way that is over-controlling, over-protecting, and over-perfecting in a way that is in excess of responsible parenting." John Ortberg, in his book *The Life You've Always Wanted*, said, "If we are parents, we want to raise our children to become mature, healthy, responsible, and decisive adults. How can that happen if, the whole time they are growing up, they never make a decision on their own and they are instructed precisely what to do in every situation— what to wear, what to eat, what classes to take, whom to date. God's purpose in guidance is not to get us to perform the right actions. His purpose is to help us become the right kind of people." Helicopter parents paralyze their kids. Fence holders empower their kids to make decisions.

First Jobs

Jobs are good. But they are bad if they: 1) Pull students away from faith-filled atmospheres. "I can't go to church because I have to pull a shift." If work regularly pulls people away from the Body of Christ, it's dangerous. I tell audiences that if you ever watch nature documentaries, you'll see that it's the little water buffalo alone at the water's edge that gets eaten by the crocodile. There is strength in the herd. Separation, especially long term, can be dangerous. 2) Jobs are bad if they create distress. Stress comes with life, and navigating stress is important for kids to learn, but there are enough pressures to be found on the threshold of adulthood. Inherent to adolescents are plenty of unique stressors. If at all possible the work grind should not be added to the list.

A few good things about working at a young age are self-evident: 1) learning to manage money; 2) learning to manage time; 3) associating hard work with remuneration which is, of course, Biblical; 4) learning to manage relationships at the work place; and 5) dealing with bosses and authority.

Submitting to and Respecting Authority

Submission is a critical aspect of society. I am founder, president and CEO of an organization for nearly a decade. I am self-employed. I joke that I work for a jerk. On occasion I fire myself, call myself to apologize, and take myself to lunch to work things out. Submission, however, is no joke. We taught the kids that even though Dad is self-employed he still has many authorities and always will; for example, civil authorities. If I'm pulled over for speeding—which may or may not have happened a few times in the last ten years—I can't tell law enforcement that I am self-employed so they should move along. I suppose I *could* tell him or her to move along and suffer the consequences. Also, I work for booking agencies, denominational leaders, pastors, organizational heads, and I voluntarily submit to my own pastor, Dr. Doug Witherup. Even the United States President has built-in systems of accountability and submission with two other branches of government.

Authority is to be submitted to and we teach that from the Bible passages that talk about it. There is safety in the submitted heart. There are those rare occasions when the individual or organization to be submitted to has invalidated the mandate. That is a reality for our children as well, albeit rare. For example, if the authority at the mall store encourages, endorses or instructs our kids to steal, authority cannot be submitted to. If the shift supervisor says, "Hey, I like you. I want you to buy these shoes, return them and keep the cash and the credit return. It's a double refund. All the assistant managers around here are doing it." Nope. If a coach is inappropriate and wants inappropriate things, that coach cannot be submitted to. They can be prosecuted. These things are understood by us as parents. They have to be understood by those we are going to give an account for that are under our authority. So, submit unless you cannot. Then, with respect and prayer, part ways, and don't roll a hand grenade in the door on the way out! Have some class and dignity. Be bold, firm, truthful and courageous, but with an honorable demeanor. That's the lesson we've tried to teach and model.

Exposing Your Kids to Conversations with Adults

As mentioned earlier, all of our moves helped our children learn to communicate with adults, particularly when same-age friendships were scarce. I have one vivid memory of Lauren as a young girl holding court with a bunch of college-aged boys. She was ten or eleven at the time. The boys were on my camp staff as kitchen workers, life guards, positions like that. They were standing around her while she sat on a picnic table, firing questions off at her about life and girls and stuff. Later they told me, "It's like talking to a full-grown lady. We couldn't believe the stuff coming out of her mouth." I always smile when I think of those days and my kids running around the campground.

Teaching Stewardship

Earlier I said that people other than me should be consulted regarding financial lessons for kids. There is one thing I'd like to offer and encourage the reader to copy as a life and parenting philosophy. We may not have a huge inheritance to pass on to our children (or we may, all things are possible). But one great gift, an inheritance of sorts, Cecilia and I have given to our kids is the wonder, the treasure, the principle and the promise of the tithe. By teaching our kids about tithing, and by modeling the principle, we have provided Joseph, Lauren, Kennon and Madeline with the ability to have all their needs met, for life. They may never be wealthy, but the promise of the tithe is that all *givers* will be *receivers*. All *blessers* will be *blessed*. Faith exercised will move all kinds of mountains, including the mountains of want, poverty and need. I can go to my grave with gratitude that this important truth was not neglected.

Extended Missions Trips

Short-term missions trips changed Cecilia's worldview when she was a teenager. They opened her eyes to a bigger world and gave her a view of what real poverty was for the first time in her life. Material possessions lost their luster and she began to understand they could never equate to happiness. Similarly, my life was forever changed in Jamaica, Paraguay, Bolivia and a dozen other countries I traveled to. We wanted that same experience for our children. Three of them have been overseas. Lauren self-funded trips to Europe that were not missions related, but I was finally able to take her on a missions trip to Asia when she was twenty-three. Thailand and Malaysia didn't reflect the poverty of, say, South America, but the countries we were privileged to minister in certainly changed her worldview. Joseph, like many firstborn kids, got to the front of the line on a few things. I took him to Asia when he was just twelve. We will never forget the midnight jungle hike in Malaysia with two hundred Singaporean teenagers. Who could forget the eerie call of monkeys in the night and wild animal eyeballs glowing at us through dense foliage?! Madeline has been to Central America a couple of times. Sadly, not with me or her mother, but they were great experiences for her nonetheless. Kennon is a late bloomer and, so far, a missions trip hasn't made it to his bucket list. Again, the concept of the "right bus" and the "right seat" from the classic book *Good to Great* applies here.

As I mentioned earlier, Cecilia and I didn't just write a check for the trips. We gave our kids opportunities to earn the money, we prayed for it, and we chipped in our part. Cecilia and I have weird feelings about people who want others to underwrite their "vision," "mission" or "calling" without making any personal sacrifices. Because these little missionaries are our kids, we put skin in the game and required the same of them.

CHAPTER 7

FUN IN MONEY MATTERS

Jerry

Financial stability is one of the most critical components to enjoying a healthy marriage. The misuse of money can create more strife and contention in marriage than any other issue that I know of. It's important that you and your spouse make decisions together as to how you will manage your income.

Consider these questions: Will you have one bank account and two debit cards? Will just one person manage the money for the family, and if so, who is the most responsible with money? Will you put money into a savings account each month or spend all you have? Will you put money into a retirement account? What about a college fund for the kids? Have you taken a look at your take-home pay and laid out a clear plan for how you want to direct your dollars? Have you set funds aside for emergencies? As we all know, bad things happen to good people. Evaluate your income, taking into account all these issues. It will help you manage your money responsibly.

The real challenge is not becoming an impulse buyer as an individual or as a couple. There are so many ads that show you what you need, but really don't need. There's always the deal of the day that makes you think you must buy now or miss a great opportunity. Are you a sucker to sales pitches for too-good-to-be-true deals?

Listen, it's easy to fall into a trap with our spending. We've all done it. I want to help you consider a few disciplines that may help you eliminate money as an issue to fight over in your marriage.

There are some great money management courses out there. Dave Ramsey has some excellent material to help you learn to budget and not overspend, and to focus on debt reduction principles. Search the internet for his teaching material. You will not regret it.

If you're currently struggling with financial issues, I encourage you to keep reading.

Financial Disciplines

I'd like to share a few disciplines Libby and I put into place that helped us pay our bills and stay out of debt even when we lived on very minimal income.

From early in our marriage, Libby and I put money aside for our kids' college funds and for our retirement. We made so little income that we didn't have much to invest, but we did invest. We also started mutual funds for each of our kids at $25.00 per month so they'll have something significant when they reach retirement age.

At one point, we made an investment in a limited partnership in hopes that the return would be sufficient that we could fund college for our kids. Some laws changed and the investment was lost. We were hurt because those college funds were gone, and one of our children was headed to college. We had to trust God for His help. Well, God is good and somehow, through a series of miracles and financial blessings, we were able to cover our children's college bills.

Let me suggest a couple of things here. First, if someone offers you an investment that sounds too good to be true, it is too good to be true. Stop now, cancel the deal and don't risk your investment dollars in a get-rich-quick scheme. Generally, the only one who makes money is the guy who came up with the idea. Stay away from quick money-making deals, because invariably you'll get burned.

Here's another tip: not every door-to-door salesman may be giving you the best advice on how to provide energy, clean water or other items for your home. I can tell you from one of my bad decisions. We had a solar heater salesman visit our home and he made it sound like a solar water heater would change our world, save tons of money, and all but print cash. I bought his sales pitch and spent a small fortune on a set of bulky solar panels for the roof of my home. It proved to be a bad decision, because five months later we sold the house because we were moving out of the area and had to pay for the solar panels with the sale of our home. Another time, a water purification salesman came to our house and tested our water. The test made it look like we were drinking toxic waste. Yet we were on city water, which everyone in town drank. We didn't buy that filter system and we are still alive and cancer free.

Libby and I have set a 24-hour rule for ourselves before making a major purchase. I suggest you do the same. Before purchasing a house, a car, a major appliance of some kind, give it some thought and prayer. The 24-hour rule allows time for second thoughts and to consider whether or not you really need that item. I can't tell you how many times we have decided against a purchase when we followed our 24-hour rule. Salesmen will say the deal is only good today, right now. So what? Pass it up anyway. They'll still have a great deal the next day if you're serious about buying. Salesmen are there to sell, so know that you are in control of your decision and you need to make a good one.

Living with Little

Most couples, in their early years of marriage, have to watch their budgets and carefully manage their funds. Typically, the income, when a couple is first starting out, is generally enough for the basics: rent, utilities, car payment and food. When we were first married and beginning to raise a family, Libby and I seldom ate out because we couldn't afford to. Libby was so good with managing the small amount of money we had for buying food, clothing or household items, but it only stretched so far.

We shopped at garage sales and bought second-hand items that became precious to us. We made some really good buys through the years and still have some of the furniture we bought in the lean days. The truth is we didn't have a choice. Our funds were limited, so we had to buy what we needed at the lowest cost possible.

We ate many meals of cereal, Hamburger Helper, and other cost-efficient foods to help make ends meet. But God was faithful and we never did without. Our kids never felt that we were living with less. They had what they needed and that was fine.

Through even the leanest of times, we were faithful in giving our tithe and giving what we could to missions, and in return God was faithful. You can trust God to see you through.

My Dad's 25% Rule

Not long after I got married, my dad took me aside and told me about his 25% rule. He said, "Son, one day you'll want to buy a house, so I want to tell you about a policy I have for managing money." He said he would only spend 25% of what he earned on his house payment. He felt this would be a good rule of thumb for me when I looked for a home. I listened and followed his rule as closely as I could. His advice helped me not let the lending agency talk me into borrowing more than would be comfortable for me with my budget.

I realize current home prices may necessitate an increase in the 25% rule to the 33% rule. But let me caution you, even if you can afford more on two salaries, there may come a time when one of you may want to stay home to raise a family or for some other reason. For that reason, I still recommend you budget somewhere between 25% and 33% of your income for your mortgage payment and no more, and hopefully you'll be able to manage your other household expenses and budget items with ease.

Everyone, at some time or another, will have some challenges with their budget. The car will break down, the roof will leak, or something worse will happen that creates a demand on your cash flow. Braces, dental work, school expenses, and all kinds of other expenses surface to put pressure on your finances. Let me encourage you to open a savings account so you'll have funds available for an emergency. I know it's hard, but with a little discipline and good luck you can do it. You'll thank me one day for this advice.

In regards to buying versus renting or leasing a home, sometimes it's best to rent or lease rather than purchase. The general rule of thumb is that if you don't plan to stay somewhere longer than two or three years, it's better to rent. The cost of the loan, the interest payments upfront, and the overall hassle of selling a home make it wise not to buy if you don't plan to stay long. Renting has many benefits. For example, generally you aren't responsible to maintain the outside of the home, nor are you responsible for maintenance if something goes wrong, such as having to replace the A/C unit or heating system.

You don't build equity or have the opportunity to see the price of homes go up, but in many market periods, homes don't increase in value much anyway. In addition, you generally pay 6% to a Realtor when you sell your home. Realtors are convenient in that they help you sell your home more quickly and save you the hassle of the paperwork and legal issues. But the downside is the Realtor's fee, and unless your home has appreciated well in the time you've owned it, that fee can really cut into your profit. You need to consider this so you can make the best decision for your family. Make your decision a matter of prayer and remember the 24-hour rule before you make a major purchase.

One of the purchases you really want to prayerfully consider before jumping in is the purchase of a time-share. Many couples have been talked into a time-share only to regret it later. Libby and I decided long ago not to buy a time-share because of the annual maintenance fees and the fact that we've had so many generous people allowing us the use of their vacation homes. We didn't want to be tied down to one vacation spot; nor did we want to go through the hassle of trading with others to change locations and pay the extra fees for those changes. I know some families who have gotten their money's worth out of their time-shares, but there are plenty of others who haven't. So don't rush into a major purchase like that. You can be pressured with "deals" that won't last. But trust me, they do. There's always another opportunity right around the corner ... if that's something that works into your budget without derailing it.

The Favor Factor

I have shared the principle of the favor of God and man for years. God's favor is amazing and we must not forget to be thankful when we experience His favor. We can also have favor with man. First Samuel 2:56 says, *"Samuel grew in favor with God and man."* Likewise, Luke 2:52 records that Jesus grew in favor with God and man. So favor with God is important, but favor with man is also important.

As I said, God's favor is amazing, yet at times it can seem unfair; it may seem that others are more blessed and favored than you are. That may be the case from time to time, but when God shines His favor on you, be generous with that favor. Give to others and share your blessings and you'll be amazed at how God continues to bless you.

Favor with man is a wonderful experience as well. Libby and I have been blessed to receive many generous gifts in our lifetime, such as the use of vacation homes, gifts for our family, and gifts that met a need when we were at a critical stage of our life.

Let me give you an example. When I was in my 30s, I went to the dentist for a check-up and he said to me, "Jerry, you need fourteen or fifteen caps if you want to protect your teeth in the years to come." I was in shock, especially when I learned it would cost between $4,500 and $5,000 dollars. (Remember this was the 80s; those caps would cost more than $8000 now.) I left his office and went to another doctor to get a second opinion. The second dentist said the same thing and that I should do many of these at the same time to keep the porcelain the same color. When I got home that day Libby and I prayed for a miracle. We made such a small salary at that time and $5,000 might as well have been $5 million. We had no way to pay that out of our budget. But within a week someone came to me and said he had been praying and God told him to give me $5,000. I almost fainted, but rejoiced as I told him why I needed the money. He was excited to know he had truly heard from the Lord and was able to participate in this blessing.

I paid my tithe on the gift, talked the doctor into a better price, and ended up with $500 left over. The dental work was not fun, but getting my teeth paid for was a miracle to us.

God has continued to bless us in the area of our teeth. I had an abscess, and another dentist made me an entire bridge—valued at $6,000—and he did it for free. He continues to be my dentist and he will not charge me for dental work. I can't tell you what a blessing it is to have people who are willing to share their blessings with us. This is man's favor on our lives.

I have also seen God's favor on the ministry of Teen Challenge. For the past twenty-five years, Libby and I have seen the organization grow from one rented facility to twenty-one facilities, in nineteen locations, in six states, housing some 1,200 students. We have experienced God's favor and man's favor. Over the past twelve years, we've had twelve one-million-dollar gifts given to the ministry. Please know that I'm not bragging, but simply trying to tell you that God's favor is amazing. We have raised more than $35 million dollars in the last fifteen years for special projects to expand the mission of Teen Challenge, both in the southeast region and globally. We don't take God's favor for granted, nor man's. We are thankful to God and we are thankful to those donors who have partnered with us to reach individuals with life-controlling problems.

My children, my board, and the staff and students have all seen God's goodness to the ministry of Teen Challenge. Those stories of God's favor and man's generosity built faith in our kids and our team. We are honored to serve the ministry of Teen Challenge and to spend our lives reaching those with behavioral and addiction issues.

The joy of giving our lives and giving of our excess is such a blessing to us. We have always shared what God has blessed us with and He has always been faithful. We can't out give God.

Joe

Financial Disciplines

As I said earlier, we have an open-door policy in our family. Anything is open for discussion. My unmarried children have access to all of my passwords. Email. Social media. You name it. They also have access to our banking information. At any time they can go into our accounts and see what we spend and where we spend it. They could see our tithing record, what we spend on entertainment, etc. But transparency is important to us, and we've used it as a teaching tool. It also serves as a convenience tool. I can instruct my kids on the road, "Yes, I give you permission to go on that outing (or get that needed item). Transfer the money from the family account to your account." Some might think that's risky. I know the children could take advantage of that kind of accessibility. But everyone in our clan knows such a transgression would be the very last time on the earth that such a transgression would occur! Transparency. Open codes, accounts and passwords.

A friend recently told me about some good advice he had been given in a counseling session. The counselor told the counselee something to the effect of: "Yes, you've done some bad things and the only thing to do now is *the next right thing.*" Nobody is perfect, that includes finances. When bad investments are made, the way of recovery is *the next right thing.* When a child doesn't tithe and finds himself outside the *"blessing of the Lord [that] makes rich, and ... adds no sorrow ..."* (Prov. 10:22, NRSV), *the next right thing* is to tithe on the next paycheck. If early in marriage a young couple made the choice to go to Disneyworld and there wasn't enough money to pay the power bill, *the next right thing* is to budget. The principle of *the next right thing* also works in our finances.

My lifelong friend Lee McBride has a term for the little things in our finances that aggravate many of us. Things like late fees, exorbitant interest rates, reconnect fees, unnecessary bank charges. He calls them "idiot taxes." I've paid my fair share of idiot taxes in my life, but when you pay enough tax of any kind, especially idiot tax, you learn a hard lesson: It hurts! So you avoid the tax at all costs.

We walk by faith and not by sight. On the evangelistic field there was no "sight" at all in the beginning. There was a weird correlation between empty calendars and empty pantries. Empty dates equaled empty accounts. I can blame falling prey to idiot taxes on my dysfunctional upbringing, but that would just be a smelly excuse. My adopted mother, Elizabeth, taught me the virtue of hard work and the value of saving money. When my parents separated, I spent one summer in Florida, working at a restaurant as a dishwasher. Mom was waiting tables. She made me save every check and not spend one penny. The day before I left for Georgia, we went to the bank and I cashed those checks to the tune of a few hundred dollars. I spent every bit of it on school clothes and basic living expenses, and didn't tithe on any of it. I didn't even know what that meant.

The Bible says that the Apostle Paul *learned* some stuff. He wrote, "*I do not speak because I have need, for* I have learned *in whatever state I am to be content*" (Philippians 4:11, MEV). I too had to learn some things. In fact, I'm still learning and growing. Our kids are learning. Even Jesus (who was and is perfect) learned. "*Though He was a Son,* He learned *obedience through the things that He suffered*" (Hebrews 5:8, MEV). Suffering induces learning. C.S. Lewis famously said, "God whispers to us in our pleasures, speaks in our conscience, but shouts in our pain: it is His megaphone to rouse a deaf world." Suffering induces learning.

In those lean, evangelistic years, our entrepreneur, Kennon, seemed to be the only one with any money. He was faithful to tithe; we all did. But Kennon was also faithful to rat-hole every penny he could earn or find on the sidewalk. It's a pretty humbling thing to borrow money from your middle-schooler to pay the light bill. I wasn't a fan of the Kennon Phillips Savings and Loan program. Kennon loved it. He knew that 1) the money would be paid back promptly, and 2) he would get a $5 interest payment on every loan. On more than one occasion Kennon asked me, "Need a loan?" Get away from me, you little loan shark! I thought right then he might become an accountant or banker, and sure enough, his majors are accounting and finance. He learned from *my* suffering. God has been faithful to us and we don't need the little entrepreneur anymore. All the kids have been privy to our family journey, including the couple of times we had our power temporarily disconnected. But as I said, God has been faithful to us, and last year alone, our ministry—not counting personal tithes, which are, of course, personal—sent $16,500 to missionaries and orphanages. That's above what we paid in staff salaries. The suffering of those early days "learned me" to build a strong intercessory prayer team, which is led by Jewell Massey. Dozens of intercessors have covered us in prayer and we are deeply grateful for that.

One funny incident about leadership, money and children involves ice cream. After a church board meeting one night that went long, I drove to my mother-in-law's house to get Joseph. He was about six years old. We drove across town to our house. We were at the light where the Magic Market convenience store was located. Little Joseph asked, "Hey, Dad, can we get some ice cream?" Very grumpily, I responded something like, "No! It's a school night. I shouldn't have you out this late in the first place. I have a huge day tomorrow and we don't have money for ice cream." Typical overreacting blah blah blah stuff parents say; grumpy dad vernacular. My six-year-old son replied, "It's okay, Daddy. I understand." The light turned green. I went through the intersection and pulled directly into the Magic Market parking lot. Like a kid would do, Joseph whipped his head around and his eyes got big and confused. "Dad, I thought you said..." I told my son that his response and his attitude just bought him some ice cream. Then I quoted this verse to him: *"From the fruit of their lips people are filled with good things, and the work of their hands brings them reward"* (Proverbs 12:14, NIV). That was a great teaching opportunity for me and a great lesson for Joseph. Look for opportunities to teach; sometimes the opportunities are delicious.

My wife and I have employed different systems of financial management over the years. For many years we had one account and two cards, which has its own challenge. My wife is a nurse. She took a break from nursing for eleven years to concentrate on raising our children (and recently stopped working at a clinic and is taking care of her eighty-seven year old mother). When she returned to the medical world after our kids were older, we opened two accounts with both of our names on both accounts. One benefit of such a system is that of tithing. I have never known a person that had such deep joy in tithing as my wife. My money is hers and her money is mine. But when a person writes a check that represents the sweat of their own brow, there's something deeply and personally worshipful about it.

As of now we have no debt except for our mortgage, minimal medical debt, and a small college loan for one of our kids. Full disclosure: One day while registering this child for college I practically emptied a pen of ink signing form after form after form. It got to where I didn't even know what I was signing! I have always tried to heed the biblical admonition to *know the conditions of your flocks and herds,* but sometimes the herd can get away from you. We really don't like debt. I especially hate bad debt. I hate credit cards. The companies are disingenuous when they tell you how much money you can "save" with their cards. One husband was weary after he heard his wife say for the countless time, "With the discount, mall bucks, and the already-great sale, I saved an enormous amount of money." He looked over the top of his newspaper, sighed and said, "Honey, I beg you to stop saving us money. I really don't think we can afford much more."

Having no debt has its trade-offs. No debt means that all four children took the same transportation to the prom. Mom's white minivan! That's a neat memory and a fun talking point at parties.

Here are some good rules about finances: 1) God first. Make it a habit to make the "first fruits" check truly the first fruit. 2) Pay yourself second.

Maybe you don't think you can afford to save ten percent for yourself. Try seven percent. It will grow quickly. Like the Bible says, little by little and you can watch your money grow. 3) Educate yourself about finances. Don't know where to start? Buy a Dave Ramsey book. Good stuff. 4) Have a budget. Budgeting our time makes our lives successful. The same goes for our "dough" and the successful financial life. Don't be a Nazi about the plan, but do have a plan. One of my favorite life verses is found in Proverbs: *"Man's heart devises his way, but the Lord directs his steps"* (Proverbs 16:9, MEV). Make a plan and listen for the line-of-scrimmage audibles from the Holy Spirit. Truly, He will direct your steps. 5) Have a reserve for the unexpected "crazy day(s)."

Here is a humorous tithing story. Kennon and Joseph, who are seven years apart in age, shared a room for a few years. One day while getting ready for church Kennon said, "How does Dad do it?" Joseph said, "Do what?" "Pay ten percent of his money Sunday after Sunday?" Joseph didn't understand the question or his brother's problem understanding the principle. So he explained quickly about tithing. Kennon said he just couldn't do it anymore and put his wallet in the dresser. After a few more questions Joseph discovered where the breakdown occurred. Kennon thought we were responsible to give God ten percent of whatever money we had *on us* Sunday after Sunday, and it was starting to hurt him. Hilarious. We all got a good laugh out of it and I instructed him that God didn't require ten percent of our *net worth* week after week, but ten percent of what we'd *earned* that week.

I was preaching in a little church in Alabama, and Kennon was sitting in the lobby, as church hadn't started yet. A little old saint—and self-proclaimed ecclesiastical cop—accosted my son while he was in the lobby looking at his phone. She was reading him the riot act for daring to look at a phone pre-service. She even played the preacher's kid card. "Your dad is the evangelist.

You should know better." Kennon respectfully responded, "Yes ma'am, but I pay my tithes online every Sunday to my home church this way. I was giving an offering to the Lord." The woman blew air through her lips dismissively and waved a hand in the air as she walked off. He could have told her he was registering to ride on the space shuttle and she would have believed him exactly the same. Kennon really was paying his tithe that way. It's his preferred method. (I like the drop method: dropping the first fruit in the bucket.) I assured Kennon everything was fine and that God would be glorified and bless him regardless of what that dear saint thought about it.

The Favor Factor

I agree with Jerry on the subject of favor. Even through the financial challenges I've experienced, it's obvious to me that God's hand has been upon me right from the start. Adoption was a mark of His favor. Right after I was adopted my dad allowed me go to a Texas rodeo with an older couple who were our neighbors. Dad gave me two dollars and I came back with five. The neighbor told my dad that people started handing me money for no reason (being a cute little three-year-old boy wearing a cowboy outfit might have had something to do with it). God helped me get through Bible school with no debt aside from $1,400 for a truck I bought just before leaving the college.

I like to tell this story when I talk on the subject of favor. Polly Hardy occupied a room at the Ralston Towers, a retirement high-rise in Columbus, GA. She was a retired seamstress and a friend of mine. When she was a small girl, she was carried by her brother and dropped. Because of that she walked with a pronounced limp, dragging her bad foot behind her for the rest of her long life. I first met Polly in a church lobby more than three decades ago when I was a teenager. I remember that meeting vividly. It followed a time of prayer in which I had prayed to the Lord something like this: "Father, I'm about to get into a 1974 Dodge Dart Swinger Special with three on the column. In two hours I have to drive eight hours due south. It will chug gallons of gas and burn half a case of oil on the way. I have five U.S. dollars in my pocket. That money won't get me out of the city limits. Since you are the one who called me to preach and go to Southeastern Bible College, I thought you should know about that." I got up from that prayer altar and walked to the lobby where Polly was standing. "Are you Joe Phillips?" she asked. She was a true southern belle and spoke with a *Mrs. Doubtfire* cadence to her voice. (Perhaps you recall the 1993 Robin Williams movie.) "I've been wanting to meet you, dear," she said. "I've heard about your dedication to the Lord and that you gave up your basketball scholarship. I've been praying for you." I thanked her profusely and assured her that I needed the prayers. She smiled and gave me my first "Pentecostal handshake." Do you know what that is? I didn't but I certainly do now. It's when you shake hands with someone and they put something in your hand. Specifically, money. Why do they call it a "Pentecostal handshake?" Well, depending on the amount of money received, a person can become downright Pentecostal when they receive it. More money, more shaking and quivering, so goes the theory. Since I wasn't familiar with the practice, I mistakenly thought she had thrust a used Kleenex in my hand. *Uh, do you need me to throw this away for you?* As she limped off I looked at what I thought was a used tissue in my hand, but it wasn't. Polly Hardy had put $100 in my hand. I thanked her in amazement, then looked at the lobby ceiling and quietly said, "From down there (pointing to the sanctuary altar) to right here ... wow! You're good. And fast!"

During the next couple of years I had some other "Polly" experiences. One day I went to box 852 to collect my mail, hoping there was a letter from my then-girlfriend Cecilia. Instead, I found an envelope from my home church, Evangel Temple. I opened it and there was a check for sixty-one dollars. I rejoiced at the surprise gift. Do you have any idea how many cheeseburgers sixty-one dollars would buy for a hungry athlete in 1983? There was another envelope that looked like the first. I thought, *this is getting more better and more better.* And it was, for that check was for $1,000! It was an anonymous donation, given through the church on a church check, but somehow I found out it had also come from Polly Hardy. Polly made quilts with her arthritic hands. She put the money she earned from selling them in a coffee can. As she collected a good amount of money she'd put it in the offering and send it to an unproven student named Joe Phillips, studying at an unaccredited (at the time) Bible college. Thousands of people have received the Lord Jesus in my years of ministry, and Polly Hardy gets a lot of the direct marketing "downline" credit for that.

That story represents favor. Like Jerry, I don't take favor lightly. The theological opposite to favor is trouble. Jesus said, *"I have told you these things, so that in me you may have peace. In this world you will have trouble. But take heart! I have overcome the world"* (John 16:33, NIV). Trouble may be inevitable, but it produces certain harvests, including evangelism. After all, the disciples went through some serious trouble which caused them to scatter all around the globe, but they took with them the message that would change the world. God works around, over and through trouble and lavishly distributes favor, and I want that favor. I don't relish the trouble that often precipitates it, but I certainly want our family to receive all the favor He wants to give.

I'm not sure we can *pass down* favor, but we certainly can *pray down* favor. An enemy of favor is fear. Fertilizer for favor is faith. I've heard that Murphy has a law. His law was never to be mentioned in our home without swift and harsh refutation. If you have never heard of the law, read this definition and then promptly forget it. Murphy's Law says: "Anything that can go wrong will go wrong." The theological antonym of this law is God's law, especially that found in Deuteronomy. *"And all these blessings will come on you and overtake you if you listen to the voice of the Lord your God"* (Deuteronomy 28:2, MEV). God has lavished upon the Phillips family His favor regarding vehicles, orthodontics, vacation spots and so many other things. There was a period of four years, early in my ministry, when I didn't buy shoes for myself. It seems there were two leaders, in two different churches, in two different states, whom the Lord assigned with the task of keeping me in new shoes. Ironically, just this week I came home to some expensive, beautiful and comfortable shoes sent to me from a preacher in the Appalachian Mountains. They were on my stoop, delivered by my postman. It is more blessed to give than to receive. We love to receive favor, but also look for opportunities to be His instruments of favor for others. As Cecilia says, "to be a blessing."

Here is a story that is so outrageous it might sound like a lie. We followed the leading of the Spirit and moved from Charlotte, NC, to Atlanta, GA. It was a gut-wrenching decision. In Charlotte, we had lots and lots of favor. In fact, that's why we moved back here after being gone for eight years. One of the greatest aspects of where we lived then was the Christian school where I worked and where our kids attended. We missed it so much when we moved. We missed the influence it had in the lives of our three school-aged kids. I took Lauren, a fifth-grader, to her new school to register. As I was registering her, there was a loud-speaker announcement that said: "Please participate in this moment of quiet reflection." We stopped registering for ten seconds. It was like a dagger in my heart. I whispered, "I hope you brought Jesus with you because that may be all of the Jesus you get today at this school." Lauren flourished, but I was concerned about the boys. I was telling all of this to the Lord one morning, and I'll never forget what happened that day. I was looking at beautiful Stone Mountain and praying. The route to work took me by the landmark each day. In the middle of my prayer for the kids and the school, I felt the Holy Spirit say, "Follow that car." The red car in front of me was turning left, and the voice seemed so real to me that I turned left and trailed the red car. I wound around, turned here and there, and finally pulled into the parking lot of one of the most beautiful churches I had ever seen, and saw a gorgeous sign that said, "Christian School." Like Philip in the book of Acts, I knew what I had to do. I went into the building and approached the receptionist. She said they only gave tours once a week and that had occurred the day before. But she gave me a packet, which I glanced through, especially the cost sheet. I wanted to say, "Oh, you've misunderstood me. I'm not trying to purchase a ride on the next space shuttle. I just want to enroll my kids in Christian education." It was *expensive.* I think the University of Georgia would have been cheaper. The hammer of impossibility was hitting me hard and doubt was beginning to fill my mind: *"Why would God tell me to follow..."* The receptionist interrupted my internal mini-crisis. "It looks like your lucky day. Here is our headmistress now and it looks like she's about to give a tour," so I joined the headmistress, Dr. Somebody or other, with the rest of the group she was leading, which consisted of just one lady. I wasn't positive, but I had the feeling the touring lady attended the church I had just started working at, which was located in another town across metro-Atlanta. I never saw her again, leaving me to wonder if I had entertained an "angel, unawares," as spoken of in Hebrews 13:2. The school was amazing, and even more beautiful than the school we had left. I walked through the halls and heard children quoting the Bible and singing about Jesus. Tears ran down my cheeks, which I hid as best I could from the tour group. It was so good and so impossible at the same time. At the end of the tour, the headmistress, who was decidedly non-charismatic and non-

Pentecostal—stopped abruptly, looked directly into my eyes and said, "I've never met your kids but I have an overwhelming impression you need this school and this school needs your family. What if we completely scholarship your boys? Would that help your situation?"

Uh, yeah. We had followed the Spirit to Atlanta, and I had followed a red car to that Christian school at the Spirit's leading. Then the favor of God followed me into that school. Lauren did well in her neighborhood school, and that Christian school was great for the boys. Amazingly, the day after Cecilia and I were elected to become youth directors for our denomination for the state of Georgia, I received a letter from the Christian school, stating, "We regret to inform you that next year we will be unable to extend the scholarships" because the funds had dried up or something. But there was no need for scholarships because we were following the Spirit to Macon, GA. Favor is timely.

CHAPTER 8

LEAVING A LEGACY
AS GRANDPARENTS

Jerry

If you're a grandparent you need to ask yourself, *how do I want to be remembered?* As grandparents we have an amazing opportunity to influence the next generation of our families. What do they see you doing that they will do after you're gone? How do you spend your time with them? If you were given the opportunity to hear what your grandchildren say about you ten years after you're gone, what would you love hearing them say?

Well, now is the time to make your impressions, now is the time to influence, now is the time to introduce them to Jesus from a grandparent's perspective, and now is the time to pass on your blessing. We will leave a myriad of memories, based on our values.

I remember my dad not wanting to spend time with his father. It wasn't because my granddad wasn't nice to his grandkids or that he didn't know how to enjoy us or entertain us. It was because he was never there for my dad when he was growing up. My grandmother died when my dad was twelve, leaving nine kids for my granddad to raise on his own. My granddad didn't take on the responsibility very well. In fact, he quickly remarried, moved in with his new wife in a house down the road, and abandoned the kids, leaving the older ones to care for the younger ones. He did, at least, leave an account open at a local store where they could get the basic groceries they needed, such as eggs, flour and a few other essentials, but that was it. As one of the oldest boys, it fell to my dad to help provide for the family. He quit school and did what he could to earn money, plus he shot wild game to feed everyone. My granddad left his legacy, but it wasn't one many would want to use as a pattern.

My granddad promised my dad things like a new bike, football or some other gift, but he never made good on his promises. For Christmas, my dad and his siblings got an orange or an apple and a few nuts. Dad never maintained a relationship with my grandfather. He did allow my granddad to take us squirrel hunting one time, but that was it, or at least it's all I remember. It was truly sad when we visited him, because he lived in a small house on a cattle farm and tended cows in the latter years of his life. He had nothing, he left nothing, and he meant little to his kids when he died. Not much of a legacy.

The sad news is that too many people have similar stories of their dads or granddads failing them or their family. It's hard to find something positive to say about them. If that's the case with you—or even if it's not—you own the responsibility to create a legacy for your family. What legacy will you leave? This is a critical question, because you will leave a legacy, good or bad. Wouldn't you prefer one that carries fond memories for your loved ones? Let's be purposeful with our lives.

Family Times

Libby has always decorated our home for the various holidays throughout the year. When the kids come into the house they ooh and aah over all of the decorations. The dining room table is always adorned with items appropriate to the holiday, such as little pumpkins for Thanksgiving, holly and candles for Christmas, and bunnies and colored eggs for Easter. We put two of our tables together, which extend from the dining room into the living room, so all seventeen of us can be together, which is very important to us.

Our nine grandkids entertain themselves at a table of crafts Libby has purchased and set up for them, which have to do with the theme of the season or holiday. The music, and the smells and anticipation of amazing food fills the house. It is moving to sit back as a father and watch your children and grandchildren interact and enjoy one another's company.

We make it a point to get everyone together several times a year and when we do it's always special. We go to the lake, and for those in town we spend Easter together. If possible, meaning if the kids find something to entertain themselves with, the adults sit around the table and talk about life, memories, and tell funny stories over coffee and dessert. Last year, as the adults lingered around the table, it cost me a 56-inch TV, as one of the smaller grandkids (we call them "the littles") threw something into the plasma TV and broke the screen. We're a bit more cautious now to be sure we know what the kids are up to before lingering around the table. But we do love that special time of sharing and being with one another.

As grandparents, how warm is your reception when the grandkids come running into your house? How do you greet them? Your reactions and welcoming spirit are quickly seen and understood. Your non-verbal communication is read by both your grandkids and your children, so be as warm as you can in reaching out to welcome them into your arms with hugs. By doing so you're creating memories and making precious impressions on those kids.

What do they see and smell when they come into your home? What type of music or TV shows are they apt to be subjected to in your company? The way your home smells and the fun things the grandkids are able to do create memories that build a sense of security and a sense of family that stay with a child for a lifetime.

Kids and grandkids need affirmation. They need you to not only hug them or give gifts, but they need to hear you say the words, "I love you! I'm proud of you! You are so special." Words last a lifetime, and you need to focus on being optimistic and encouraging to your kids and grandkids. I'm going to repeat myself: Affirm your kids and grandkids! It's critical to good emotional health and well-being.

Selfishness is what stops many from saying nice things about their kids or grandkids. When someone is so consumed with being right, or so consumed with their own world that they can't reach out to others, that's selfishness. Some become so health conscious or weight conscious that they can't do anything but point out the negative things about someone else, which can devastate the one to whom it's directed. I see this all the time with those we work with, and it's so sad. Please take a moment right now and call your children and affirm them. Call your grandkids and tell them you love them. Get past yourself and your schedule, you're not that important in the scheme of things, so take a moment to reach out.

Paw Paw's Personal Devotions

Every morning I'm up early doing my devotions before the Lord. When the grandkids are at our home, if they get up early they'll find me reading my Bible or praying. They generally come to where I am and crawl up in my lap. I'll keep reading for a while, even reading aloud to them until they get restless. I pray with them and ask them who they want to pray for, which is always interesting. Often they will ask, "Whose Bible is this, Paw Paw?" because they know I have written some thoughts in a Bible for each of them.

Here's how that happened.

When my oldest daughter was sixteen, I began to think of her going to college and I decided to take one of my Bibles and write notes to her all through it as I read it that year. I told her I was praying for her and that I loved her. Through my notes I would speak into her life and encourage her to take a close look as she read. I would be in different parts of the world and would write things like, "Today I am in Prague, I prayed for you today." Or, "I'm in Moscow, what a pretty city. Denee', I love you, I'm proud of you, I'm praying for you today." Sometimes I dated the entries, sometimes I didn't.

When she left for college, I wrapped it up and gave it to her. I realized I had started something, since I have two other children. I started on another Bible for Kristi, my second daughter, finished it, then moved on to a Bible for my son, Dustin. All the while, I spoke into their lives as I read through their Bible. It became an amazing discipline.

A few years later, I had my first granddaughter, so I bought a Bible for her. I have followed the same process now for my eight granddaughters and one grandson. Over the years, I've bought Bibles in different colors for the girls. I bought one granddaughter a pink Bible and carried it for a year. I can tell you I got plenty of interesting looks when I'd use it for a speaking engagement. I'll never forget when I spoke in Poland at the Teen Challenge 25th anniversary celebration. I carried my pink Bible with me to the podium. It just so happened I wore a pink shirt which matched the Bible. I didn't intend to do that, but somehow there I was with a pink Bible and a pink shirt. I explained that the pink Bible was for my granddaughter and the practice I had for leaving something inside for each of my grandkids.

Everyone understood and appreciated my commitment to leaving each of them a legacy in the word of God. At lunch that day in Poland the wife of one of the leaders said she was glad I explained the color of the Bible because she thought maybe I was just carrying a pink Bible to match my shirt. We all laughed and I told them that a man has to be comfortable in his manhood to carry a pink Bible. But one day my granddaughter will read the thoughts and prayers her granddad had for her and it will be worth it. May God use those Bibles to keep my grandkids close to the Lord and to living by the values declared in God's word.

The legacy we leave as parents and grandparents matters. Our heritage is a valuable part of our family life.

Sleepovers at MeMe's and Paw Paw's

We often have the joy of the grandkids staying over for a night or sometimes several nights. We do our best to make it fun and enjoyable for them. Libby is so good with the kids and always has things for them to do. We often let them "camp out" in sleeping bags in the family room. They so enjoy lying out in the den, watching some children's movie, and getting to sleep all together on the floor.

When the weather is right we may even sleep on the screened porch with the kids. We have two outdoor couches around a mobile fire pit. Libby and I get the couches and the kids put their sleeping bags wherever they find room. We are fortunate to live a short distance away from a wildlife refuge which makes our yard quite interesting. We often see deer, raccoons, squirrels, possums, turkeys, and other critters strolling through the yard. As it begins to turn dark, we even see bats flying around the yard—which is one reason it's nice to have a screened-in porch. The sounds of the night are always interesting. We love to hear the wind blowing through the trees, and love seeing the moonlight. It's such a cozy feeling to be out there with the grandkids, talking quietly to them before they drift off to sleep. We have a great time "camping out" together. It's a really special time when we light the fire pit, make s'mores, laugh and tell stories. These kinds of times are priceless and build great memories for our grandkids—and for us as well.

Teaching the Grandkids to Hunt and Fish

I'll never forget the day I had four of my granddaughters digging for worms in a pile of woodchips. We were going to fish off of the dock and needed fresh bait. The girls weren't the least bit intimidated and had a blast digging them up and putting them in plastic buckets. When my son-in-law saw what was happening he was shocked to see his daughters digging through the woodchips for worms. He said, "Paw Paw, look what you've done to my daughters!" They had so much dirt under their fingernails, and their hands were filthy. But they loved it and so did I. We caught a lot of fish that day. And now that they're older, if they want to fish off that dock they know how to find worms!

I also love to hunt deer. I've taken my son hunting every year since he was twelve. We go every opening day, which is usually the weekend before Thanksgiving, and we go throughout the season every chance we get. We always have a great time. It never dawned on me I'd have the joy of taking my grandkids hunting, but last year my ten-year-old granddaughter Aniston and my nine-year-old granddaughter Avery went with me. I dressed them in some of my camo and put hats on them so they felt like they were really hunting. It was quite a challenge keeping the girls quiet and focused on looking for deer. They actually brought their iPads to play games on while they waited, which was a different kind of hunting experience for me.

My deer stand holds two people comfortably and I had one girl in the extra chair and the other on the floor playing with the iPad. They'd change positions every so often, taking turns playing with the iPad and sitting in the chair, hunting. I took drinks, candy, and other snacks to keep them occupied.

We were lucky and saw several deer come across the field in front of us, and I shot an eight-point deer that day. We waited about fifteen minutes, then we went looking for the deer, which had run into the woods after I shot it. I knew I hit it by the way it jumped, and I knew it couldn't have run very far. As we entered the woods Avery was glued to my leg while Aniston ran ahead of us. I kept reminding her to stay with me as we looked for the blood trail, because there were all kinds of dangers out there in the woods, such as snakes and critters, not to mention a wounded animal. Avery, on the other hand, would hardly let me walk she was so close to me. We searched for a while but couldn't find the deer. I decided we had entered the woods a bit too far down from where the deer had disappeared, so we searched in another area and sure enough, twenty steps into the woods, we found it.

Aniston saw it first and squealed. She was so excited to see we had gotten the deer. Avery was still glued to my leg. She finally relaxed a bit and went to look at the deer. We took it to the processor's shop and they got to watch as it was gutted. You should have seen their eyes and heard all the "yucks" that came from them, but they watched the entire process. I mounted the horns for Aniston and she put them on the wall in her room. I took far more photos on my iPhone than necessary, but I wanted to document that wonderful experience. I guarantee they'll both tell their version of this story the rest of their lives. These kinds of activities will build lasting memories that I pray will always bring a smile to their face.

We were hungry when we left the processor's shop, so I took them to a local spot I like and broke them in on hot wings. Now, every time we pass the place they mention the day we ate wings there after hunting. It was so much fun. They both fell asleep on the way home, mouths open, their heads leaning against the windows. It was a picture I'll never forget. What a day!

Of course, my daughter and son-in-law loved that the girls had such a great time. This will likely become an annual event, and I'll do my best to turn all my granddaughters into hunters. Watch out, boys, they may shoot better than you do.

Speak Blessings over Your Kids and Grandkids

If you get any advice out of this book regarding your family, I hope it's this: Speak blessings over your children and grandchildren. There are biblical examples for us to follow. Isaac blessed Jacob; David blessed Solomon. These men of God spoke words of faith, hope and love over their children that God honored. Their blessings entailed enormous responsibility for Jacob and Solomon, but also came with enormous influence and wealth. I'm not saying your child or grandchild will have the responsibility of Jacob or the wealth of Solomon, but we do need to bless our offspring.

To bless our children is to affirm them by telling them how much we love them, how proud of them we are, and by speaking life into and over them. You might say something like: Denee', or Kristi, or Dustin, I'm proud of you, you are such a joy to your mother and me, and I'm asking God to bless you and keep His hand on you and give you success in every area of your life. I ask God to add his favor on your life and to grant you the desires of your heart. I pray you use the gifts and talents God has endowed you with to the best of your ability. I'm impressed with your level of maturity, and it's a joy to see you step into God's plan for your life. I pray you never back off of anything you believe God is asking you to do. I pray you keep your prayer life fresh and that you go to the Lord in prayer every day. Spend time alone in His presence and be all you can be for Him. I bless you! I bless you in your going and coming. Know there is nothing you can do to diminish my love for you. Go now and live in the blessing and favor of the Lord.

You may want to write out your blessing then speak it over your child.

Assure them of your love and respect for who they are and what they have become. Remember not to put *your* goals or *your* aspirations on them. They have to live their own lives and find how their individual gifts need to be utilized. Just bless them, and trust God to honor that blessing.

Joe

<u>Family Times</u>

I literally owe my life to my aunt, who talked my mother out of terminating her pregnancy. She became my grandmother after adoption. I truly loved my grandmother and grandfather. Both are now long gone. Cecilia lost her grandparents long ago as well, so I never had a chance to meet them. She did meet mine just before they passed. A portrait of her mother's mother, Cecilia's Nana, hung for decades in their den. Her legacy was reinforced every day for Cecilia and her sister.

We are recently discovering the joys of grandparenthood, just days into it as of this writing. I don't really know what to expect. Everyone, and I mean everyone, tells us how incredible it is to be a grandparent. When people ask me if I am excited, my standard answer is, "I have a Shih Tzu poodle. I love that dog. Is it better than having a dog?" People's body language changes dramatically at the reply. They aggressively tell me the sheer joy of what it is to be a grandparent and many tell us the standard jokes that go along with the job. You've heard them. "It's God's reward for not killing your own kids." Stuff like that. I have never once met a person who reported, "You know, it's kind of a drag being a grandparent."

I do know that my mom, Elizabeth, and Cecilia's mom, Anne, have had a tremendous impact on their grandchildren. Jimmy, Cecilia's father, left a great mark as well, on all of us in fact. I loved him a great deal, so much so that I dedicated my first book to James A. Griggs. The following is an entry written by Jimmy's oldest daughter—and my wife—Cecilia.

> *My grandfather left my dad and his mom during the Great Depression. They were very poor and had to rely on the kindness of friends for housing, although my grandmother, Elizabeth Hamilton Griggs, worked very hard as a seamstress. My grandfather was not a good dad to my dad. He was not a good role model as to what a good father, husband and citizen looked like. He was an alcoholic and made promises he didn't keep. My grandmother went to a tent revival led by evangelist Mordecai Ham and accepted Christ as her Savior. Mordecai Ham is the same evangelist that led Billy Graham to Christ. Life changed when my grandmother became a follower of Christ.*
>
> *My dad strayed from Christ during his teenage years. He married my mom on July 25, 1959. I was born in 1961, and my sister, Julie, in 1966. In 1968, my mom was diagnosed with a brain tumor. She had surgery to remove it, but when the surgery was complete Dr. Hazouri said, "No hope." She was alive, but in the natural there wasn't much hope. My dad went to the chapel to pray, promising God he would quit drinking and serve Him the rest of his life if God would spare his wife.*
>
> *God did work that miracle—my mom is now eighty-seven. Our whole family accepted Christ as our Savior as a result. My dad changed. He quit drinking. He would say in his testimony that he was a working alcoholic. He quit*

smoking cigars. He was a new creation in Christ.

My dad was an amazing "Daddy," though it had never been modeled by his own dad. He loved my mom with his words and actions. He told my sister and me often how much he loved us in words and actions. He became a great prayer warrior.

My dad changed. Yes, it's possible. He became a great husband to my mom, and a great dad to me and Julie. No, he wasn't perfect but he chose Christ daily. He changed, and because of his decision to follow Christ every day of his life as his mom had done, the course of history changed. I am a third-generation follower of Christ because I chose Christ for my life. All four of my children have made the decision to accept Christ as their Savior.

What a great legacy James Griggs left for his children and grandchildren and future generations.

Papaw's Personal Devotions

The moral of that very personal story from my wife is that it's never too late to create a legacy. The man my wife just honored had an extremely well-attended funeral. I was especially grateful considering the funeral was conducted during football season on a Saturday in the Deep South. If the reader knows anything about SEC football, that testimony is well understood. Let's just say people plan their week around football games. I was so proud of both our daughters, who spoke at the service. Their words were amazing. They took the job seriously. Honestly, I tried to discourage them from speaking. I wanted them to have the freedom to simply grieve. They both took speaking at the service as an assignment, a mandate. Legacy, a word that Webster defines as "something transmitted by or received from an ancestor or predecessor," demanded the honor of my children.

Sleepovers at Nana's and Papaw's

Recently my daughter showed me a picture she keeps in her phone. It's a photo of papers. It looks to be about sixteen pieces of paper spread out like playing cards. They are the prayer lists of her grandparents. The lists are long and frayed at the ends. The handwriting is both Nana's and Papaw's. Some of the pages are so worked over they look like they were written on ancient papyrus. Since Jimmy's death, Anne has kept alive the imperative of prayer. She is very dedicated to her nighttime routine of reading the Word and praying.

I remember walking into Nana and Papaw's room to say goodnight when they visited us or when we visited them. As they got older, sometimes they didn't respond to my knock or "good night" because age had diminished their hearing. So I would peek in to check on them. An image is indelibly printed on my mind of the two of them in prayer. Anne's head would be on Jimmy's chest while they prayed for what seemed like hours per week. Sometimes during the prayer Jimmy would look at his papyrus sheet and bring the next request: "Dear Lord God, I bring..." He brought hundreds, perhaps thousands of people and requests to the Lord. I've called the kids to the door before to give them a visual of what legacy looks like. Those prayers made a difference to so many. In fact, I'm still reaping the rewards of the prayers of a man now in Heaven. Legacy prayers from legacy people have very, very long shelf lives. Cecilia and I hope to live up to that kind of legacy for our children and grandchildren.

Speak Blessings over Your Kids and Grandkids

There is great power in our words. Much has been written about the power of the patriarchal blessing. There are rich examples in Scripture about the blessings of elders. The New Testament has powerful insights about our words. Insights like: *"Out of the same mouth proceedeth blessing and cursing. My brethren, these things ought not so to be"* (James 3:10, KJV). *"From the fruit of their mouth a person's stomach is filled; with the harvest of their lips they are satisfied"* (Proverbs 18:20, NIV). One definition of "curse" is "a prayer or invocation for harm or injury to come upon one." There is a difference between "cussing" and "cursing." Cussing is bad words. Cursing is bad business; bad family business; bad policy and bad destiny.

For ten years I've made it a habit to bless my kids at the end of my prayer time. I speak them, write them or type them. My confessions are enumerated in detail in my book *The Third Chair: Implementing Lasting Change*. The blessings related to family are these: My children all love God and they are going to serve Him all the days of their long lives. My children's college education is already paid for and some of those college-educated kids are going to come back and work with their dad. My marriage is fruitful and prosperous like a fruitful vine.

I don't believe the words are some kind of magic formula, some mystical "Open Sesame" incantation. I do believe this constant reminder to my spirit calibrates my own faith. Faith opens doors and moves mountains. My expectation is set with these regular reminders.

Words live. My cool grandfather, whom I mentioned earlier (he became my great-grandfather through adoption) said something to me decades ago I haven't forgotten. I played one year of college basketball on scholarship and my major was pre-law. I was one of the few members of the family to attend college. When I told my grandfather I was going to be a lawyer he said,

"Good! This family could use a good lawyer." When I later told him that God had called me into the ministry, he was profoundly disappointed. He spent some time thinking about it and the next time we spoke, he gave me this blessing: "I've been thinking about it and I know that if you're going to be a preacher, you're going to be a good one because you have a winning way with people." The Bible says, *"A word fitly spoken and in due season is like apples of gold in settings of silver"* (Proverbs 25:11, AMP). Without knowing it, my grandpa, Clessie Rollin Mills, gave me an ornamental apple of gold that day. I put that apple on a shelf in my mind and pick it up on occasion to remember and admire. He gifted me with that blessing. When you bless your children and grandchildren, be careful. They might actually believe the blessing and do great things for God.

CHAPTER 9

PARENTING:
WHAT I WISH I HAD KNOWN!
WHAT I'M GLAD I KNEW!

Jerry

What I Wish I Had Known!

At one time I believed that parenting responsibilities ended when the kids left for college or got married. The truth is that's a myth. You never stop being a parent. I'm not complaining, I'm just stating a fact. Your kids will always need you and you will always be involved at some level in their lives.

My dad had the conviction that when you turned eighteen you went to work and left home. I don't hold that conviction but I did have the illusion that our kids wouldn't need us in the ways they had when they were living at home. That's not to say they are needy or that they're not grown up and doing well, it just says parenting doesn't stop when they leave the house.

We've found that our kids do need us and want our input just as much now that they are away from home as they did when they were living with us. The conversations are different but the parenting continues. This isn't a burden; I'm just saying that you will parent your children until you breathe your last breath. I happen to like being needed and I love it when I can guide my adult children through any and all of life's situations, but I want to be there for them only when they want me to be. I also enjoy my daughter-in-law and my sons-in-law and appreciate when they come to me with a question or two. It's rewarding to know you've learned a few things that might save your kids some pain. To be needed or sought out for wisdom is rewarding.

I wish I had realized that just because your child marries a wonderful person it doesn't mean they won't have problems and face challenges in their relationships. I wish I could spare my children financial challenges and the challenge of health issues for themselves or their children. As parents we need to let them deal with their challenges and not enable them by coming to their rescue in every situation, but there will be times they'll need our help, and we can always offer counsel, support and input.

Libby and I have tried to help in ways that will enable the kids to provide things for their kids, our grandkids. In the early years of marriage, money is generally tight and it can be challenging to pay for all the extra activities kids are involved in. We decided we could help by sending them a monthly gift to pay for piano lessons, sports programs and other activities. In doing so we take some of the pressure off our kids in a tangible way that also helps our grandkids. We won't need to do this forever; we just happen to be in a place where we can help a bit. These are ways you too can help your adult children without giving them permission to be irresponsible with their finances. You may have other ways you help your adult kids, and that's wonderful.

I wish I had understood sooner what's meant by the saying, "Life is messy." I have learned that we all have a measure of pain to manage at some point in our lives. That pain can come in so many forms: health issues with your child or grandchild, your children's relationships with their spouses, or their financial crises. There are many other things to challenge the myth that when you get older, life gets easier. I've come to believe that life provides different kinds of stress, pressure and pain all along your journey. How you handle that stress or pressure is what matters the most.

I wish I had known earlier in my life that, rich or poor, everyone experiences challenges and pain in life. Money helps with some situations, but in many of life's challenges, no amount of money can help the situation or lessen the pain. If you haven't already learned this, let me pass along this lesson: we will all go through some crisis at some point in our lives, so don't get discouraged or believe that God is picking on you. Just realize it's part of life, and trust God to help you through.

I also wish I had known that appliances don't last forever. More than likely you'll have to purchase more than one washer and dryer set in your lifetime and more than one refrigerator. Things break down, and usually at the worst possible time. We learned this after returning home from a week's vacation, when we discovered that our air conditioner and refrigerator had broken down at the same time. It so happened we had a freezer full of fish and game at the time. When we walked into the house we were met with a swarm of flies and a smell so bad we almost gagged. A pool of blood and decomposing meat had run down and through the entire refrigerator and covered the kitchen floor. It was the worst appliance breakdown we ever had. I can't think of it without remembering the horrible smell and the flies. And the clean-up? It was awful.

Hopefully, you'll never experience something quite that bad, but I can almost guarantee you'll have something break down at the worst possible moment. There's never a good time for a car to break down or a major appliance to quit working, but it almost never fails that these kinds of things happen when you're short on excess funds and when you least need another challenge in your life.

I wish I had known that when my kids came to me with a problem,

problem solving wasn't what they wanted most from me. What they needed most from me was to listen. I had to learn this, and as a type-A, driven person who solves problems all day long at the office, when approached with a problem at home it was easy to jump into the problem-solving mode. It was tough for me learn the difference, still is. Listening is so critical, especially when you have teenagers.

I wish I had known early on that "going shopping" had a different meaning for women than for men. Shopping is more like hunting than you might think. You go with your wife or daughter to look at a blouse in one store, they try it on, ooh and aah over it, they really like it, but don't buy it. Then they take you to another store and do the same thing. You may go to five or six stores in different parts of the city to finally come back to the first shop and buy the original blouse you saw. I wish I had known the process and said no to the shopping trips. I have learned to ask more questions about where they want to shop and will commit to take them to only a certain number of stores then I sit in the mall walkway areas on a bench where I read or watch people. I can do that and be happy, but standing in the women's department while my wife is in the changing room has never been my idea of fun. I'll do it occasionally and try my best to occupy myself without looking like a weirdo in the women's department, but it's a commitment. I actually wish they had a seating area with a TV tuned to a sports channel to watch while the ladies shop. That might get more men to go hunting for clothes with their mates and children and ultimately boost sales.

Finally, I wish I had known that words from Dad can really impact your child's self-esteem and that those words can encourage or discourage them in ways you never imagined. Dads need to understand how important their approval is to their children, especially their daughters. Even as adults, how you react to their decisions, purchases, schooling, clothes, haircut, etcetera, is important. Be careful with words and do your best to be attentive to them. Just because you have an opinion doesn't mean you have to express it. We need to manage what we say to our kids. Dads, Moms, your kids need your approval in their adult lives as much as they need it in their childhood. I'm still learning that.

What I'm Glad I Knew!

I'm glad I knew how important it was to spend time with our kids while they were young. It created a relationship between us that opened lines of communication that continued into their teen years and beyond. I'm glad I took time to play with the kids and enjoy playing catch, kickball and other games when they were young. I enjoyed being in the swimming pool with them and playing board games with them. Those times built such good memories. I knew this because my dad played ball in the back yard with me and my two brothers. My dad never missed one ball game my brothers and I played. He and Mom were at every event we had in school and I'll never forget that. That's why I knew it would be important to my kids.

I'm glad we turned off the TV at dinner time and that we made it a point to talk and discuss the day's events.

I'm glad I knew how important missions trips were to our teens' development of their worldview. I knew this because of my own experience as a teen going on a trip with a group of church kids. Feeding the homeless, teaching children and sharing my faith with others was life-changing for me. I knew it would be for our kids as well.

I knew we needed to have family devotions and pray together as a family. I knew this because I grew up in a family that prayed together. I never left home for school that we didn't stop in the kitchen, bow down and say a word of prayer before leaving the house.

I'm so glad I knew that taking two weeks of vacation each summer would be good for us. Even though this wasn't something I did in my childhood, I knew I needed the time away to truly relax. It was a renewal time for me, and the kids loved our vacations. As a family we would start talking weeks in advance about what we wanted to do that summer. The kids would get so excited and make all kinds of plans for our trips. We especially enjoyed our beach times together.

I'm also glad I knew the joy of giving, and that teaching the kids to give would be so valuable to their lives. Our kids are generous today as adults and I'm so proud they embrace this value. I can only pray they will teach their own kids to do the same.

I'm glad I knew that disciplining our kids was good for them. Kids need boundaries and parents are the ones who primarily own this responsibility. These boundaries impact how we treat one another, how we address adults, how we act in school, church, and in public in general. Children need our guidance in setting boundaries for them. This brings security for them and helps them mature into adults with a sense of integrity, honor and respect for themselves and others. I'm so glad I knew this was important. I knew this because of the Bible's teachings on this subject, but I also knew because I experienced discipline and boundaries from my parents when I was growing up.

I'm thankful I learned a healthy fear of God and kept myself pure prior to marriage. In our culture, that kind of commitment is not the norm. However, I continue to believe it's important for our kids and grandkids to keep themselves pure for marriage. This is one of the greatest challenges for youth today, but will be one of the most rewarding for them if they commit to it and succeed.

I don't want to make anyone feel less successful as a parent if this wasn't your life experience. I get it, no condemnation from me, but why not encourage your kids and grandkids to take the challenge? I'm just glad that a healthy fear of God kept me in line. I truly didn't want to disappoint God, and I also felt he would judge me if I did. That may not have been such a great thought about God, but it helped keep me pure.

I'm glad I learned a good work ethic as a child and teenager. I had chores from the time I can remember. I had jobs earning money and was taught how to save and manage my money. I'm so glad these life principles have helped guide me as an adult. I owe so much of the success I have experienced in life and personal finances to my parents' teaching, and especially to my job at my dad's store selling shoes. Among many other things I learned to speak to adults and to be responsible to an employer.

I'm thankful I learned at an early age to be hospitable. My parents welcome people into our home and I witnessed them being good hosts to our guests. I believe we should treat others as we want to be treated and be welcoming in our daily lives. Hospitality is a gift we give to others. Being warm and friendly makes a difference in how we experience life. As parents we set the tone in our homes. Our kids will pick up on how we speak about the pastor, our boss and our neighbors. My parents never spoke ill of others as I was growing up. They weren't critical of any one in front of us. If they had issues with someone, they talked about it in private.

These are things I wish I had learned before parenthood and a few things I already knew. You might consider how to apply these lessons; it may be that you make a few adjustments in your behavior and parenting.

My goal is to encourage you and give you food for thought as you practice your role as a parent. May God help you and bless you in your efforts. May he give you the wisdom and discernment needed for each situation you encounter. Stay strong, stay focused, spend time in prayer and

God will help you make the right decisions. Trust me, I've done it, and I'm still doing it.

Joe

What I Wish I Had Known

There are so many things I wish I had known. My heart is glad that someone as smart as Dr. Jerry Nance admits he could have done better too. I have a philosophy that we can only operate within the light that we are given. I hope this book serves the purpose of giving you some more light. As of this writing, the Golden State Warriors and M.V.P. Seth Curry are on pace to possibly win more basketball games than anyone in the history of the NBA, including Michael Jordan's Chicago Bulls. Currently, Golden State has a winning percentage of 0.914. They are 53-5. That is practically perfection. Statistics bear out that baseball players with the most homeruns often have the most strikeouts. Parenting is not for the faint of heart. All perfectionists, be on alert: there will be a few "L"s in the Loss column. I've had my share of "L"s.

I wish I had known earlier about the power of words. We have two sets of kids, so to speak. Boy, girl came along first. Then four years later another boy, girl born nineteen months apart. I thought I was being funny when I'd say I had the "A Team" and the "B Team." Years later I stumbled upon the fact that the statement "B Team" was offensive. I had to apologize. I understood. A Team is the starting five, the elite. B Team was the practice squad and often the scrubs. I never meant it that way about my kids. I meant it in a chronological way. All I could do was apologize and do the *next right thing,* which was to remove it from the lexicon. I've never said that again.

I wish I had taken more *real* vacations. I wish I had taken *longer* vacations.

I wish I had budgeted better and saved more money. I have such an aversion to tightwads and parsimony that I may have swung the pendulum too much the other way. I wish I had known about Dave Ramsey.

I wish I had camped with the family.

I wish I had known about the Five Love Languages much earlier.

I wish I had gotten into hunting and fishing.

I wish I had a different paradigm on family devotions. I was nervous that perhaps the kids would rebel if our devotions were laborious and legalistic. The old adage is true that the plumber's pipes are never fixed. The kids were in good and great churches. They were mostly educated in great Christian schools. We prayed with the kids always and often, but I think I could have been more creative.

I regret I didn't take the youngest three on missions trips with me sooner and more frequently.

What I'm Glad I Knew!

I'm glad I understood the power of the "door-knob" prayer. I have always and without exception prayed for the anointing of God to preach, lead meetings, go on missions trips and outreaches, but the most important ministry that can happen in my life happens within the four walls of my home. So it's worth praying about. When my hand reaches the doorknob at the end of the day or after a trip, I pause and thank God for his special anointing to love the most important people in the world to me. Those are worthwhile prayers.

I'm glad I went to a men's retreat in 2009 I vehemently did not want to attend. God got ahold of my life on Joy Mountain, NC, in a profound way. One of the retreat exercises was to do word carving. On an 11-inch piece of wood I carved the word "Legacy," the name Cel with a cross, and the letters J,

K, L & M. I keep that piece of wood on top of a stack of Bibles I've read that sit on my dresser. I'm glad I have that visual reminder to try to live in a way that leaves a legacy for the ones I love.

I'm glad we taught our kids to be generous. My youngest daughter told us that God once told her to empty her savings account for a single mom with cancer trying to raise two small children. She had just met her. She said, "God told me to give her $300 for her kids' Christmas." She would not be dissuaded. I told her to take a few days to pray about it to make sure it was from the Lord. We knew it was God when she said respectfully, "Dad, do I need to get a cab and go to the bank myself? The Lord told me I had to do this, and I'm willing."

I'm glad we understood that at some point our parenting relationship would transition from being God-ordained authority figures to the role of providing our children with the wisest counsel we could offer.

I'm glad we understood the transforming power of love. Truly love does cover—and did cover—a multitude of sins, offenses and wrongs (Proverbs 10:12; 17:9; 1 Peter 4:8, NIV).

CHAPTER 10

LAUGHING MATTERS

Jerry

In this final chapter I want to share some funny stories of things that have happened to me and a few others on the road of life. I've been through so many situations that make me laugh; I hope my stories will bring a smile to your face. Hopefully you can look back at a few of your own stories and find things to laugh about. Whether you laugh or cry is really about perspective and how willing you are to look on the bright side and let things go.

A few years ago I went to visit the Teen Challenge center in Moscow, Russia, and had a great time with the students and staff on that visit. A few months later I was speaking in a conference just outside of Moscow, and the director of the center I had visited asked me to baptize seven of his students. I failed to ask some critical questions, like is this going to be indoors? Will the water be heated? And how does one dress in your culture when you do your baptisms? Those were key questions I learned through that experience.

I can tell you're getting ahead of me, and you got it, it was outside in a lake that was Antarctic cold. The nights got down to 32 degrees, literally freezing cold, when I was given the honor of baptizing those students. There were about 150 family and friends who attended the event. We walked down to the lake where I discovered that those of us participating in the baptism were to wear long white robes—which I also discovered were paper thin, meaning you could see through them. I looked through the available robes for one that was large enough for me and happened upon a couple that were thicker than the others, so I quickly claimed one.

There was a changing booth on one side of the lake where you could undress and change into the robe—while your legs were exposed at the bottom of the changing booth to the 150 people standing there waiting. I finished changing, gathered my courage and waded into the lake, thinking it would be deep enough fifteen to twenty yards from the shore to do the baptisms. No chance; it was at least seventy-five yards before it was deep enough to baptize anyone. In no time at all my legs began to freeze; the deeper it got, the colder I got. My only consolation was that it shouldn't take more than twenty minutes to baptize seven people. Once again I was wrong.

Sergei, the director of the center, decided to sing a chorus in between each person being baptized and he gave them each an opportunity to testify. That meant three to four minutes between each song and three to four minutes between each person's testimony. Before it was over I spent an hour in that water. My friends were on the shore smiling from ear to ear as they watched me shivering in that freezing lake. It wasn't so funny to me at the time, but now I laugh every time I remember it.

On that same trip I had a friend traveling with me who was on his first missions trip. We stayed in a hotel just across the street from Saint Basil's Cathedral, and every time we came out of the hotel a group of gypsies would come up to us to beg for money. They would even follow us for a few blocks and continue to beg. Well, my friend Cliff made the mistake of giving a few rubles to some children, which attracted more. But what really increased the number of beggars who followed Cliff was something I did. You see, Cliff was a black man with a shaved head who looked a bit like Michael Jordan. So I told the beggars instead of begging from me, they should go to "Michael Jordan." From then on, they mobbed Cliff every time we left the hotel, with the crowds growing bigger daily. A few days later he asked why so many beggars mobbed him and left the rest of us alone. I said, "Black people are like rock stars in Russia ... but it may have something to do with the fact that I told them you're Michael Jordan." He couldn't believe I had done that and then he began to laugh. So did the rest of us and we laughed until we cried. It was just my way of breaking Cliff in as a world traveler.

Another funny story came about when I was a pastor. I'm convinced God uses certain people within the church to keep pastors humble. I know every pastor who reads this will agree. I was the pastor of a wonderful church, and we too had a couple of "special" members. One day as I was walking out to the platform I noticed a lovely new couple who looked like accomplished business people. They were first-time visitors and I was happy to have them with us. They sat on the fourth row and settled in for the service.

As fate would have it, my special church members, Benny and Elaine, sat down in front of them. When I saw this, I began to pray, hoping nothing would go amiss during the service. Well, Benny must have had a runny nose because he pulled out his handkerchief. He not only blew his nose but he made a long drawn-out blowing sound that was just outrageous. Then I watched as Bernie opened the handkerchief to look at his accomplishment. But that wasn't enough. All of a sudden he said to Elaine in a really loud voice, "Look, Elaine!" to which she responded in an even louder voice, "Eeeeeuuuu, Benny, that's grrrrooooooss!" The lady sitting behind them turned pale and closed her eyes. You got it, they were up and gone as soon as the service ended and I never saw them again. Like I said, I'm convinced God uses incidents like that to keep us humble.

Another funny and rewarding incident happened one day as I was going into a Teen Challenge center to teach a class. I had just climbed two steps and reached the landing to go into the building when one of my staff stopped me.

He had graduated from our program, attended a staff-training school in California for a year, and had returned to join our staff. To my amazement he proceeded to complain about how badly I was running the ministry and how everything that Teen Challenge in Southern California did was the right way to do it. He said I needed to know that I was doing everything wrong. He just kept going on and on, telling me how much better things were in California. I just stood there listening—I'm convinced God gave me extra grace that day.

As this staff member continued to complain, a bird landed in the tree above his head. I hadn't noticed the bird, but suddenly it unloaded an unbelievable amount of bird dropping on this guy. It hit him just at the top of his forehead and ran down to the end of his nose. He stopped talking, while I did everything I could to keep from breaking out in a belly laugh. Somehow I managed, but I couldn't keep quiet. I said to him, "Don, when God sends a bird to poop on your head, maybe He's trying to tell you to stop complaining." Don didn't say another word and as he turned around to leave I said to him, "Hey, Don, just thank God that cows don't fly." He didn't find that humorous but I sure did. I've laughed at that story for years and used it as an illustration when I speak about those who complain. Believe me, it translates well into every language. So may I offer a suggestion? If you're going to complain about leadership, you may want to avoid standing under a tree … not that God couldn't have a bird bomb you anyway.

Early on in my leadership of Teen Challenge we needed to locate a property for our program. I looked at buildings and properties all over the Orlando, Florida, area. A Realtor showed me what seemed like a hundred places and none of them fit our need. One day my Realtor called and said there was a new listing on the market that I might want to see. I met her and her associate on the steps of a seven-building office complex. As we were about to enter the first building one of the ladies said she was told that in the year that the property had been empty, snakes had taken over. I instantly looked down to see if there were any snakes to be seen, and thankfully there were none. I wanted to appear manly and said, "It's daylight. If there are snakes around here, we'll see them. Let's go on in." So we toured the property, one building after another, and I could literally see our organization occupying each of the buildings and could envision a use for every space. As we were leaving the third building I opened a door to step outside when I heard a loud scream, then felt a snake land on my neck. It had been sleeping on top of the door and when I pushed it open the snake fell down onto my neck. I began to dance, slap and run all at the same time, doing whatever it took to get that snake off me. I had no idea what kind of snake it was, but just the fact that it was on my neck made it deadly as far as I was concerned! When I was certain it was no longer on me, I looked back to see what happened to it. Thankfully, the door had slammed on it and it was dead, hanging a foot from the ground. I kicked it into the bushes then went to find the Realtors, who had run away, screaming. But now they were laughing at me for how I had reacted when the snake landed on me. And they couldn't stop. I was still a bit petrified so it took a while before I could laugh at the situation.

You'd think that was enough excitement for one day, but no. The entrance to the next building brought another bit of excitement. Having just had a snake on my neck, I was looking all over the ground for anything that slithered. Not seeing any I began to pull on the door. The lock was tough to open so I jiggled the door a bit, and then another scream came from behind me. I looked up and at the top of the door was an enormous wasps' nest. I had stirred them up and they were flying right at my face when I turned to run. I got stung once, twice, three times on my back before I hit high gear, thinking if I could outrun these two Realtors, I'd be fine. They escaped without being stung, and again they laughed until they cried at my expense.

I tell you, I'll never forget that day. And in spite of the trauma, we bought that facility, and hundreds and hundreds of men have found Christ and freedom from addiction at that site. To this day I can't walk the grounds of that facility without thinking of snakes and wasps. But I do laugh about it now.

One of my Teen Challenge director friends, Wayne Keylon, told me about the time a donor called and offered to provide the center with some turkeys for Thanksgiving. Wayne thought, as I would have, *Butterball turkeys, nice large packaged frozen turkeys.* He sent a few of the senior students in the program to get the turkeys, say thank you, and share their testimonies with the donor. When the boys knocked on the door, the farmer said, "Come on around back and we'll get the turkeys." So they followed him "around back" … where he pointed out two live turkeys in a pen. He said to the students, "Go on in and get them." The students asked, "How exactly do you get them?" With that, the farmer handed them a two-by-four board and said, "Hit 'em on the head."

The two boys started toward the pen, scared to death, not knowing that if those turkeys felt threatened they'd become aggressive and try to spur them, which would not be a good thing. But they went in and the fight was on. They chased those turkeys all over that pen and finally knocked them senseless. They put them in the back of their station wagon and headed back to the center, but halfway home the turkeys woke up and went crazy in the car. They pooped all over everything and ran around in circles all the way back to the center.

When they arrived, the boys parked the car and went inside. Wayne asked, "Where are the turkeys?" They answered, "In the car. They're alive and we're not messing with them again!" So Wayne got a group of boys with bats and boards to circle the car. He pulled open the back door and once again the fight was on. Eventually they took the turkeys down again and took them into the kitchen. The cook had never plucked a turkey before and when he pulled the feathers out of the first one it woke up and ran all over the kitchen, knocking over pots and pans, but finally the cook won the battle. The turkeys were dead, but the story lives on.

I've learned the hard way to ask questions—lots of them—when someone calls and offers us this or that. Questions like, "Is it alive?" "How big is it?" "How old is it?" "Why are you giving it to us?" I hate to offend anyone, but trust me, I don't need another turkey story.

My brother told me of a time he went to the Little Rock Zoo with his daughter. Terry and McKenna were eating peanuts as they strolled through the park. When they got to the part of the zoo that housed the big cats, one of the zoo workers warned them not to flick any of the peanuts at the panther. They continued to look at the cats as the worker moved on to another area of the park. Terry saw a group of boys go up to the cage where the panther was. She was lying down, minding her own business, when the boys—who had not gotten the same warning Terry and McKenna had—started tossing peanuts at her to try to get her to growl at them. She sat up and began to growl lightly, then she began to pace around her cage. She paced for several minutes as the boys continued to flick peanuts at her. Then all of a sudden she backed up to the fence and blew panther poop all over them. It sprayed them from head to foot. Those boys stood there in shock, trying to figure out what had happened to them, while Terry and McKenna laughed till they cried. The moral of the story is: Don't flick your peanuts at the panther!

These are some of my favorite stories. I'm sure you have your own funny stories as well, because *laughing matters* happen to us all.

Joe

All of my kids are really fun and they are really funny. They use their wit freely. When my son married my beautiful daughter-in-law, Chelsi, she had quite an adjustment to make as she settled into our family. She is from the Appalachian hills of Southern Ohio. She had one brother growing up and her dad was and is a very successful coal barge captain. Her house wasn't as loud as ours was. Our tables were occupied by so many stand-up comics—my wife is hilarious in her own right—the meal experiences sometimes seemed like a competition where everyone was competing for the stage with their next quip, impersonation or monologue. Anyone joining us for a meal could be overwhelmed to say the least.

"A merry heart does good, like medicine." So says Proverbs 17:22 (NKJV). I could write a treatise on just the dumb stuff I've done. My truck began to stink so bad one time I'm surprised the neighbors didn't complain. Every day the truck smelled worse. I looked everywhere to figure out the problem and finally found the culprit. When I unloaded Cecilia's groceries one day I didn't see a package of meat, which eventually slid between the seat and the door in the backseat of the truck. This happened in south Florida where it's a thousand degrees outside under that hot sun every day. Whew!

Cecilia once purchased something for the house at a home-decorating store. We had six humans in the minivan along with lots of luggage, but she found two topiary trees at a great price she just had to have. There was no place inside the van to put them so we wrapped them up and tied them to the top of the van. We were getting the "skunk eye" on the interstate and people were grabbing their children's hands while clutching them close at rest stops. We couldn't figure out what was up until someone said, "It looks like you have two dead bodies on top of your van." Yep. It sure did.

We did our best to raise our kids without cursing them ... and without cussing as well. We were successful for the most part. I have a sermon I preach about Ehud, the left-handed hero from the book of Judges. I conclude that sermon by saying that Ehud changed an entire generation because of one decision and the land had peace for eighty years. That's 29,200 days of peace because of one decision. (You can read about Ehud in Judges 3:12-30.) Then I say, with some bravado, "My children have never seen their dad smoke a cigarette, drink a beer or heard him say a cuss word." Not long after preaching that sermon the family and I were driving through South Carolina to get home after Easter vacation. It was the middle of the night and the family was sleeping. I had stopped for gas and had purchased a steaming hot cup of coffee. Trying to be quiet, I put the cup in the van's cup holder, but in the process the lid popped off and coffee splashed out and scalded my hand. The carnal nature buried deep in all mankind came out of my mouth in that moment. I let a word slip out of my mouth that used to slip out BC—before Christ. The word is in the Bible and it rhymes with Sam. It has an alternate meaning of a structure that holds back water. I didn't think anyone except the Spirit heard me say the word, which I had whispered under my breath. But before I could even repent, my oldest son said to me in a groggy voice from the backseat, "Streak's over." I knew in that moment Proverbs 16:18 was absolutely true: *"Pride goes before destruction, and a haughty spirit before a fall."* That's what I got for bragging. The streak ended that day, but I immediately started another long streak.

Keeping with the inappropriate language theme, here's a story throwing Mom under the bus. Cecilia and I were engaged in a vigorous discussion one night as we pulled into our driveway. What we were talking about escapes me, but I remember I said something in a smart-aleck fashion, and under her breath, Cecilia called me a name. That word is also in the Bible. It's used for a farm animal and rhymes with class. Lauren, who was nine at the time, heard it and said, "Mom, you said a bad word! How could you do that? You're a preacher's wife!" Cecilia shot me a look that basically translated, "This is your fault." I know because I've translated that look many times throughout our marriage. Cecilia sheepishly apologized to Lauren and probably justified it with, "Your father drove me to it," or some such thing. But Lauren wouldn't let up. "I've never heard you do that. You should have known better. I don't understand." She walked down the hall to our room firing off these admonitions until Cecilia had simply had enough. She said, "Alright, I have repented and apologized to God, your father and the family. Are you going to forgive me or do you think I'm just going to have to go to hell?" To which Lauren simply cocked her head and held up two fingers. In other words saying, "That's two, Mom. You going to go for three? Where will it end?" At least that's how I read it. Those two fingers and the head tilt have made us laugh dozens of times over the last sixteen years.

To round out the cussing segment, here's a story that took place the day after Christmas one year. Cecilia and Joseph, who was five years old at the time, went to take back some Christmas presents. They were in a long return line at the local department store. The line was so long it literally came out of the back of the store and was queuing up on the sidewalk. Cecilia was holding Joseph's hand but he stepped away from her for a second to get a good look at how long the line was. He looked to the front of the line, then up at his mom. He looked again as far as he could see, then back at his mom. He did this a third time, then in a loud voice he said, "Mom! What the ..." Again, a Bible word and it rhymes with smell. Everyone around them heard it and laughed with a laugh of relatable sentiment. Cecilia's eyes got as big as saucers. She was going to have to stand in line with these people for the next hour! When Cecilia got home we launched an investigation. Joseph hadn't heard those words at home and certainly not at Nana and Papaw's house. Finally we discovered the source. It was a line from the Christmas movie, *Home Alone*, which we wore out that season in an ancient device known as the VCR. What a lesson that was to us. Kids are sponges. Protect the sponge!

I ran an errand at the mall once and took Joseph with me. Again, he was about five. As we walked back to the car we stumbled across a scene at a hair salon at the mall. People were gathered at the entry way, watching and listening as a disgruntled customer yelled at the cashier, reading her the riot act. The crowd was really getting into it. It was surreal. I, myself, was in awe that a bad haircut could elicit that kind of raw emotion. It was getting ugly, so it was time to go. As I looked down to tell Joseph we had to get out of there, my heart fell to feet. He wasn't beside me. I looked around frantically and then I looked up to see that my five-year-old son had navigated through the crowd and was just a few feet away from that crazed customer. Before I could part the sea and race through to snatch him up, something hilarious happened. During the only lull in the tirade—perhaps while the parties were catching their breath—Joseph looked right at me, which meant he addressed the entire crowd, jabbed his thumb over his left shoulder, and said, "Dad! Blabbermouth!" The crowd broke out in laughter, which I took for my cue to snatch up my son and run for the car.

Trying to get the kids to bed was always an adventure. It seems like Jerry and Libby had a better touch than I did. I don't recommend the following story as a parenting tip. One night after putting the kids to bed and listening to them carry on for much too long, I reached my limit. I walked to the foot of the stairs and yelled, "That's it. Enough! If I hear one more word from you boys, if I have to say one more thing, I'm coming up there to knock your heads off!" (Please don't report me. They knew I was exaggerating. And the statute of limitations has expired.) Kennon, who was probably in third grade, slipped out of bed. Joseph said. "Get back here! Dad's mad and he isn't kidding. He's gonna come up here." But Kennon ignored him, and rummaged around in the closet, making enough noise that it made Joseph even more nervous than he already was. He whispered louder, "Get back in bed and be quiet!" At that, Kennon emerged from the closet wearing a football helmet, and climbed into bed. "Knock my head off, will you?" he said. "Try it now. I'm geared up." They both laughed into their pillows—and laughed their heads off.

Kennon was our most unique kid to potty train. He's smart but he didn't take to the *geography* of the training program. He didn't wet his pants. He did, however, wet other things. The babysitter couldn't find him one night. She looked in every room and finally came into the kitchen where she found the refrigerator door wide open, the vegetable crisper open, and my son watering the veggies in a perfectly unsanitary way. On another occasion we were in a Hall of Fame induction ceremony for Papaw. Jimmy Griggs was being inducted into the Columbus State University Hall for being a superb broadcaster and for being a great supporter of the university. Of course, everyone was dressed in suits, ties, and nice dresses. When it came time for the family to gather for a photograph I couldn't find Kennon. The room where we were gathered had one glass wall, from floor to ceiling, which overlooked a courtyard. Clustered near the wall were five little old ladies looking at something. "Oh boy," I thought, as I walked over to where they stood. Looking over the tops of their heads, I saw a little boy on the sidewalk, with his pants around his ankles, his back to the glass, making an impressive arc. I muttered aloud, "There's a kid with no home training. Probably his mom's fault." The women just looked at me with their hands to their lips, grinning. I walked over to Cecilia and said, "I found your son. He's watering the sidewalk."

Cecilia joined us for our large, weekly, pastoral lunch one Tuesday, and brought the babies with her. Kennon was still in the midst of potty training, and in the middle of lunch he said to his mom, "Got to go. I go by myself!" We were seated in a room that was a new addition to the restaurant, and the restrooms were located in this new addition. So Kennon proudly went to the restroom by himself and promptly began to sing at the top of his lungs. We knew this because the acoustics to the new wing hadn't yet been refined. When it was obvious the concert wasn't going to end anytime soon, I stepped away from the table, where my colleagues sat laughing, to ask Kennon to be quick and quiet, then I rejoined them at the table. Things were going well until all of a sudden Kennon exclaimed, "Ooh, two doo doos!" The ministers at the table began to laugh again, unable to stifle it. I closed my eyes and hung my head, and just when the laughter subsided, as if on cue, Kennon loudly observed, "Two doo doos. A butterfly and a rainbow!" More laughter.

Kennon did some other things as a child related to bathroom humor. We were on an elevator with the general superintendent of an entire protestant, evangelical denomination, when the superintendent bent over to give little Kennon a special greeting. He told him how cute he was, and after he stood up and faced the door, cute little Kennon "set one free," as my friend Lee would say. Yep. Little Kennon blew the trumpet. All eyes were on the doors, though there were grins on some of the faces. Another time, on an elevator in Orlando, FL, Kennon saw a famous basketball player named Dikembe Mutombo. Little Kennon said, "Hey, you're Dickie DiBumbo." The African athlete, a former great player, grunted something neither Joseph nor Kennon understood and bowed his seven-foot-two-inch frame and shook Kennon's hand, which actually wrapped around his entire arm.

We were driving the I-285 loop in Atlanta, and Kennon, who was five at the time, let out a blood-curdling scream. I turned around and saw blood everywhere. It looked like he was in the squared circle, up against a pro wrestler. Here's what happened. Kennon was taunting three-year-old Maddie, calling her a name she didn't approve of. Not a bad-word name, just a name she didn't like. She said, "I told him three times not to say it and he said it again." So she smacked him in the head with a seatbelt buckle. Because the blow landed near the hairline, blood flew everywhere. We pulled into the parking lot and correction was administered. He hurt less in the end than Maddie's hind-end hurt, I can assure you. She never did that again.

One time Joseph got a care package at college from his precious Nana, Cecilia's mom. She has one of the most giving hearts of anyone I know. Joseph was excited. Every kid loves to get care packages at college. He wondered if it would be cookies or money, or both. Joseph has some girth like his dad. He saved the package so he could open it in class, adding to the anticipation. But when he opened it, his excitement turned to disappointment, then to laughter. Nana is the champion prayer person in our family and the top giver, but since the surgery Cecilia mentioned, Nana doesn't always have a filter. (Once after I had slimmed down a little, Nana saw me and said, "Joe, I believe every time I see you you've lost more and more"—I sucked in my gut, pushed out my chest, smiled, and waited on her to finish the sentence— "hair.") Joseph tore into his care package to find that his Nana had sent her firstborn grandson several articles on weight loss. "I was going to send you some sweets but I thought you'd like this instead." Her good intentions and his cookie disappointment yielded a funny story. We all love Nana!

Each child really is different. Our Maddie is a little quirky. She once wore a Valentine's Day apron on stage to lead worship. It wasn't even Valentine's Day. The difference between Kennon and Madeline was vividly demonstrated one day at a Hospice House. Cecilia and I told the kids, "We're going to see Mr. Jess and he's going to heaven soon. He'll look different than you remember him, and he won't know you're there. It's okay if you don't want to go in; you can wait in the lobby if you'd like. It will be perfectly fine." We went into the beautiful Hospice House on the Ohio River, in Huntington, WV, with our two children in tow. It was definitely a different kind of visit. Maddie walked directly up to a dying man who was hours from the "death rattle" and completely incoherent. She smiled, rubbed his arm and said, "Hey, Mr. Jess, it's me Maddie. You're gonna get to see Jesus soon, aren't you so glad? We will miss you." Cecilia wiped a tear, looked around and said, "Where's Kennon?" I told her he took two steps into the room, looked at me and said, "I'm out. Where's the vending machine?"

Once I took the kids on a working vacation, which means I did all the work. It was at a camp in North Carolina. Cecilia stayed home and worked. The day after the camp, we were going to go to the beach, so I dropped Lauren off to order fast food while the rest of the tribe went next door to a department store to buy beach towels. I pulled up to the door of the department store and gave Joseph cash. "See how fast you can get some beach towels and sunscreen." In the five minutes it took him to make the purchase, a man perhaps in his sixties and a young teenage boy got into a fist fight in the parking lot. I got out of the car and walked over to the action while Kennon yelled after me, "Dad, what are you doing!?" The older man was reaching for a knife when I grabbed both of his wrists, looked him in the eye and said, "You better go." "The punk started it!" he yelled. "Is that going to be your story when the police get here? And they are on the way." As he walked off, the foul-mouthed kid started taunting him and cussing him. About that time the mother of the teen pushed up a grocery cart asking frantically, "Hey, what's going on?!" There was another taunt and litany of cuss words from the kid and his brother. I loudly and firmly told them to shut their mouths. I said, "Ma'am, this boy just fought a man with a knife on his belt and won, this time, but if he doesn't learn some self-control he's going to wind up in jail or worse. It was an old man today, but one day it will be the wrong old man." "Get your *bleep* in the car *bleep, bleep, bleep*!" she screamed. I reached my car as Joseph was climbing in. Kennon said, "Joseph, Dad just broke up a fight in the parking lot!" "What the heck!?!" Joseph said. "I always miss the good stuff." "It was awesome," Kennon said. "Dad used his angry voice."

I held my firstborn son in my arms one night as we walked into church. Cecilia and I were having a disagreement. I can't remember what we were arguing about but the memory is vivid. Cecilia turned to make a point and started laughing in my face. Now ladies, that is not a winning tactic in arguments. No man likes to be laughed at. As her laughter became uncontrollable I looked down at my nice, white shirt to see that my son had pooped all over it. As soon as I saw it, I busted out laughing as well. That scene at the threshold of a church is a metaphor for family life. Poopy situations are inevitable. If we can learn to laugh at them, lean into faith and love each other, everything is going to be alright.

A Final Thought

I took Kennon with me on a road trip during spring break one year. I wanted to play some basketball with my son so we went to a local YMCA. "We used to be members of the Y in West Virginia," I told the attendant. "I'm currently not a member of a Y," I continued, "but I'd like to play ball for a couple of hours with my teenage son. Can I pay a fee of some amount?" The worker told us that the county was on spring break and it would simply be impossible. "There's not a gym in Muscogee County that will be available." I furrowed my brow and said, "Huh." We were disappointed. Before walking out I leaned over the desk and quietly asked, "If I give you $1,000 could we play today?" The clerk thought for a moment, and said, "Yes, of course." I practically shouted my response to Kennon. "Hey, son, did you hear that? He said it was impossible, but where there's a will, there's a way!" I turned back to the attendant and said, "Thanks for the information," and we took off. On a whim I took Kennon to the local university. We walked in to that amazing and new complex and found the bust of Papaw on the Hall of Fame column. I secretly hoped that might give us some leverage. We found our way to the athletic director's office. I introduced myself to the receptionist and asked if we could play on a practice court or something and inquired how much it might cost. The athletic director overheard from his office and walked out. We introduced ourselves to him but he said, "I know who you are." "You do!?" "Yes, I was the girls' basketball coach here when you played in the 80s. I knew your father-in-law as well." We had some nice conversation then he gave us the keys to the kingdom. We had ten brand new baskets to ourselves for as long as we wanted. We had all the fantastic basketballs we could ever shoot. Just like that, we went from "no gym in the county" to the best gym in the region. Keep plugging with your family. Nothing is impossible with God.

I preached in Arkansas once and during the message an illustration came to me. I talked about domino artwork. Like me, you've probably seen 10,000 dominos or more set up in a vast warehouse. It can take days to put the configuration together. When the front domino is tapped, the remaining dominos cascade into each other, sometimes in breathtakingly creative ways. I asked the congregation that day, "Do you know what messes up the program, what ruins the run of dominos? It's when one of the dominos is too far back from the others." Then I quoted this verse: *"Now unto him that is able to keep you from falling, and to present you faultless before the presence of his glory with exceeding joy ..."* (Jude 24, KJV). One of the fellas in the crowd that night went to the local store and bought a box of dominos. He told me later he carries one in his pocket all the time as a reminder that he's the guy too far away to fall in the long lineage of family that has fallen. If you have just graduated from a rehabilitation program and wonder if you can make it, I encourage you to put a domino in your pocket. You can surely do it, just like Caleb of old. *"Caleb silenced the people before Moses and said, 'Let us go up at once and possess it [the land of Canaan], for we are able to overcome it'"* (Numbers 13:30, MEV). I have since brought dominos on stage and showed audiences the "mess up." We want to mess up Satan's plan as he uses us like his toys. A contractor in North Carolina heard the illustration and got a tattoo of a domino that spanned his shoulder. I'm reporting, not endorsing. Lee McBride says in his presentations, "Hell had a staff meeting. The devil screamed, 'We had Joe Phillips! Who didn't do their job? He was on his way to the abortion clinic. Somebody ruined it. He got poor and bitter. We had him. Who dropped the ball? He was deep in sin and hopelessness. Somebody is gonna pay.'" You and your family might wind up on the agenda at one of Hell's staff meetings, but with Jesus you can be the domino that doesn't fall. Everyone in front of you can fall into addiction, depression, hopelessness, lovelessness and despair. But Jesus can keep you from falling. Just like in a domino art project, if you stand, everyone coming up behind you can stand too.

My cousin has never met my family. We hadn't seen each other in decades but we reconnected recently. We had a few phone conversations. During one conversation my cousin was talking about the extended Phillips family and said, "Drunk, drunk, drunk. It's a Phillips thing." I let that comment slip. Then he said something about prison, "You know how the Phillipses are." I let that pass by as well. But the third time he referred to calamity as the "Phillips way," I interrupted. "I have to stop you here for a minute. You've referred to abhorrent behavior three times as the Phillips way. If you made those comments to my four children, they'd look at you like a cow looking at a new gate. They'd have no reference point for what you're saying. They're smart kids, but they wouldn't connect the 'Phillips way' with prison, perversion and addiction. We're not better than anyone else, including members of the Phillips family. However, because of Jesus, when you say the 'Phillips way,' to them it means, 'blessed when we lie down; blessed when we rise up; blessed going out; blessed coming in.' It means love, favor, faith, blessing and destiny." So I ask, what does the "(insert your last name) way" mean? With God's help you can be the domino that changes the "way" of the domino effect on your family because Jesus is the Way, the Truth, and the Life.

Jerry

I pray that Joe and I have given you some food for thought. We've tried to be transparent as we shared about our values and the principles we used in parenting. We've given you a glimpse into our lives and homes and I pray that the principles we've shared will help you. We all have different journeys but we have a loving God who is ready and able to help us as we depend on Him for guidance. I give much of the credit for our beautiful children to Libby; I'm sure Joe would say the same about Cecilia. We are not done yet. We have so much more to give to our family and are committed to pressing on and finishing well.

May God bless you and may He enable you to find peace and favor as you walk out life with your family. Remember to laugh … and shut off the electronics in your home tonight and enjoy one another.